In memory of Eb —

A Century of Excellence

Golden Valley Golf & Country Club

by Rick Shefchik

© 2014 by T. Eliot Press. All rights reserved.

No part of this book may be reproduced in any manner without the express written consent of the publisher, except in the case of brief excerpts in critical reviews and articles. All inquiries shall be addressed to:

T. Eliot Press
P. O. Box 1119
Pinehurst, North Carolina 28370

First edition published 2014
Printed and bound in Canada

10 9 8 7 6 5 4 3 2 1

Library of Congress Control Number: 2014940841
ISBN: 978-0-9794836-2-2

Book and cover design by Ben Hood of T. Eliot Press
This book was set in Garamond, Avenir, and Palatino Linotype

Part Six color photographs courtesy of Peter Wong Photography with the exception of hole number fifteen. All other photographs in Part Six courtesy of Golden Valley Golf and Country Club.
Golf course rendering by T. Eliot Press.

TABLE OF CONTENTS

PART ONE	*My Golden Valley*	9
PART TWO	*Left Behind*	17
PART THREE	*Hard Times*	33
PART FOUR	*The Shriners Take Over*	61
PART FIVE	*Country Club*	77
PART SIX	*The Golf Course*	105

FOREWORD

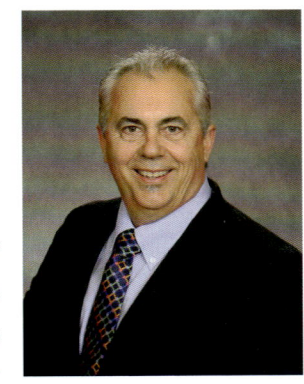

It's with my sincere appreciation of all that has been done before me that I try to put the last hundred years in perspective. There have been thousands of members before us and there will be thousands more in the future. Our founders had the foresight to purchase this amazing piece of property and to select A.W. Tillinghast to create a distinctive championship golf course that challenges players of all abilities. They've continued to enhance our country club experience by adding amenities and building one of the finest clubhouses in the state. The members before us have created an atmosphere of openness and friendship that is famous. Members and their guests are continually amazed at the love and respect that we have for one another, as they experience the true friendship that we've developed over the last century.

Our membership is very proud of this golf course and it shows in the way it's continually updated and maintained in accordance with A.W. Tillinghast's vision. Every time we step on this course, our expectations are high. We eagerly anticipate our legendary golf tournaments like Golden Days, Valley Days, The Tillinghast Cup, The Club Championships, and The Iron Man. We walk around the clubhouse and see all the history of those that have won these tournaments before us. We dream about winning that tournament some day and becoming part of that history. When we win and get our name on the wall of fame, it's a distinct feeling of pride and accomplishment, knowing that we will always be part of the rich history and traditions of Golden Valley. When we come up short, we walk off of this course and wonder what could have been. We always look forward to the next time we get to play Golden Valley and we never, ever get tired of playing this masterpiece of a golf course.

We are honored to be the caretakers of this this history and the great accomplishments of those that came before us. Our members have created an environment where you always feel warm and welcome. It doesn't matter if you're stopping by to swim, play tennis, hit a few balls, have a quick bite to eat or play this stunning golf course. It's a place where you're always greeted with a smile. As our past members and employees strove to make Golden Valley the kind of place where friendships last a lifetime, we strive to deliver on our core promises to our members now and for generations to come. I hope you enjoy our book and look forward to helping you become part of our tradition.

James M. Brown, Jr
President, Golden Valley Golf and Country Club

Golden Valley Golf and Country Club
Aerial Photograph: May 8th, 1947
Courtesy: United States Geological Survey

PART ONE ~
MY GOLDEN VALLEY

Odds were long against the golf club at Golden Valley surviving its first year, much less reaching its 100th anniversary. Time and again over the Club's first century, it faced adversity and prevailed:

- Most of the initial members abandoned the original Golden Valley site to create a new club in St. Louis Park.
- The first golf course had to be redesigned several times.
- Three times the Club had to financially re-organize.
- The first two clubhouses burned to the ground.
- Bassett Creek frequently flooded parts of the course.
- Extraordinary financial help from members kept the doors open during the depths of the Depression.
- The post-war economic boom could not save the Club from being sold.
- There was a contentious transition from a men's golf club to a family-oriented country club.
- Expanded access rules for women had to be crafted to reflect the times.
- The Club's core asset, its magnificent A.W. Tillinghast golf course, had to be restored to its original greatness after years of misguided tinkering.

The list of challenges was a long one, but at every turn, and with every crisis, the golf club at Golden Valley emerged stronger and more focused. What has been forged over the past century is a club of deep tradition, values and vision. After surviving so many crises, the Golden Valley Golf and Country Club is a place where a problem is seen as an opportunity, and change is progress.

And all along the way, succeeding generations of members have had a hell of a good time.

The birth of Golden Valley Golf & Country Club dates to 1914, when a group of Twin Cities businessmen surveyed the local golf scene and determined there was room for another private golf club.

Golf in Minnesota had begun two decades earlier at St. Paul's Town & Country Club with a crude five-hole course laid out in a farmer's pasture near the Mississippi River. Golfers from Minneapolis gradually took to the game as well, at the city's first golf course, Bryn Mawr in 1898, and a year later at the new Minikahda Club, created by former members of Town & Country. From there the game spread to Interlachen Country Club (which opened for play in 1911), and to the White Bear Yacht Club, which opened its first nine-hole course in 1912.

In 1913, twenty-year-old American amateur Francis Ouimet stunned the sporting world by defeating British superstars Harry Vardon and Ted Ray at the U.S. Open in Brookline, Massachusetts. His victory made headlines around the country and stoked the golf fever that was growing in virtually every city. Once thought of as a rich man's game – though it had its origins among the shepherds of Scotland – golf was suddenly seen as a healthy form of outdoor recreation that could be enjoyed by anyone, providing one had access to a course.

Both Minneapolis and St. Paul were forging ahead with plans to open the state's first public courses: Glenwood (now Theodore Wirth) in Minneapolis and Phalen in St. Paul, even as more private golf courses, such as Woodhill Country Club, Rochester Golf Club and the University of Minnesota course, were being conceived and built. Just as Minikahda's full membership led to the creation of Interlachen Country Club, Interlachen quickly filled its own roster and started a waiting list. Passionate golfers were again looking for a place to play.

A series of informal meetings at the West Hotel in Minneapolis brought together grain merchants, bankers, lumbermen, salesmen, lawyers, doctors, real estate brokers and other businessmen who wanted to start a new golf club. Though these meetings were not documented, early members of what became the Golden Valley Golf Club dated their organization's beginnings to these meetings, first held in 1914.

Potential members were recruited and sites west of Minneapolis were explored – sites that were becoming more accessible as houses, neighborhoods, roads, as well as rail and street car lines, continued to push into the western suburbs. Plans came together on February 1, 1916, when accountant Charles A. Tardiff, a former member of Interlachen, convened a meeting of seven businessmen: himself, lumberman P.M. Parker, railroad man William N. Cavan, insurance man Edward Von Ende, salesman Arthur C. Statt, steel broker Walter I. Fleck and R. O. Johnson to formally organize a golf club and embark upon site selection.

The group rounded up thirty prospective members by the time of the next meeting a few weeks later. Statt, a 31-year-old traveling stationary salesman from New York who moved to Minnesota in 1911, was a member of the committee appointed to find a site for the golf course. He reported that an ideal site had been identified: a 138-acre parcel of pastures, cornfields, woodlands, hills and wetlands in Golden Valley. The land consisted of two adjoining farms owned by William Varner, Sr., and son Clark Varner. The site was reasonably accessible by a gravel road or by the Minnesota & Western Railroad, both of which traversed the property. The easiest access to the property was to board the train at the station on 7th Street North in Minneapolis and get off at 19th Avenue North, at the old farm house that was used for the first clubhouse.

One of Two Varner Farmhouses on Original Property
Courtesy: GVGCC

WILLIAM VARNER, GOLDEN VALLEY PIONEER

William Varner moved to the Twin Cities from Ohio in 1854 with his wife, Louisa, and sons Alonzo and Clark. After first residing near St. Anthony Falls, he set out one day to find a permanent home site to start a farm and raise his family. Heading due west, Varner passed lakes, marshes, fields and woods until he'd walked more than seven miles to the foot of the highest hill he'd yet encountered. Climbing the hill, he stood at the top and gazed at the green valley beyond, filled with golden daffodils. He vowed to return to the spot and settle there with his family, in "my valley, my Golden Valley." Varner brought his wife and sons to the site, built a log cabin, and homesteaded the land.

The hilltop on which Varner stood is now the site of the Golden Valley Golf and Country Club. Native Americans had once hunted buffalo below the hill that eventually became the sixteenth green, but Varner was at the vanguard of a group of white settlers who would transform Golden Valley into an agricultural area.

William Varner's Log Cabin on Original Property
Courtesy: GVGCC

In those early days, neighboring settlers would gather at Varner's home during hostilities with the local Indians, but eventually Varner became friends with the original inhabitants of the land. An Indian helped carry a deer Varner had shot back to the cabin, and when the Indian expressed amazement at how sharp Varner's knife was, he let the Indian sharpen his knife on his sharpening wheel. More Indians came to Varner's house to sharpen their knives, and solid relationships were formed.

Varner was one of several Golden Valley men who served in the Eighth Minnesota Volunteer Infantry when the Civil War began in 1861. He remained with the unit through the end of the war and then returned to Golden Valley, which was incorporated as a village on December 16, 1886. On January 3, 1887, Varner became one of the first elected officials of Golden Valley, along with his son, William H. Varner, Jr. He served two terms on the council.

Golden Valley consisted primarily of farms, mills and dairies until the Electric Luce Line Railroad came through the village in 1912, bringing with it residential development. By that time, Varner had passed on, and his heirs decided not to keep the farm going.

When William Varner died in 1907, his family put the original 133-acre homestead up for sale. The site committee came to an agreement with the estate's administrator to pay $500 per acre for the land, with $60,000 to be paid in twenty-year bonds at six percent interest.

With a site selected, all the Club needed now was enough members to generate the necessary funds to proceed. It was determined they would need 100 members to get the Club off the ground. At the Club's first open meeting on July 8, 1916, 68 men signed up at a $25 initiation and a $30 annual membership fee. It would be called The Minneapolis Golf Club, a name that had been briefly used by the golfers at Bryn Mawr, but was now available (Bryn Mawr had been plowed up for home development in 1909). A membership committee was formed to recruit the needed members, and three days later the Club filed articles of incorporation.

The Club elected St. Paul lumberman Hendrick Booraem as its first president. The vice president was R.O. Johnson, Charles A. Tardiff was secretary, and Ed Von Ende was treasurer.

Golden Valley's First President

Hendrick Booraem was a native of Jersey City, New Jersey, who moved to St. Paul in 1905 to take a job as bookkeeper for Abbott Manufacturing Co. An ambitious man, Booraem soon struck out on his own in the lumber business, first forming the Halsted-Booraem Lumber Company with Hugh Halsted, then becoming manager of the Booraem-Powell Company, hardwood wholesalers, with offices in the Lumber Exchange Building in downtown Minneapolis.

The business was a success, and he married his first wife, Beatrice Louise Fletcher, in 1910. They had two children, Hendrik Hank Booraem IV, born in 1911; and Fletcher V. Booraem in 1912.

Beatrice Booraem died in February 1916. By that time, Booraem had developed a passion for golf. He carried an eight handicap, was a member of Golden Valley's first five-man team for the State Amateur championship of 1917, and faced the Club's best player, Ed Longley, for the Director's Cup during Golden Valley's first full season. He was selected as the Club's first president.

Hendrick Booraem
Courtesy: Minneapolis Morning Tribune

Booraem remarried in October 1917, to Mary Hewson. By 1920 he was president of his Minneapolis lumber company, and took his younger son Fletcher into the family lumber business. Older son Hendrick III, who was prepped at The Blake School, graduated from Columbia University and remained in New York for a distinguished career in theater, radio, television and advertising.

Hendrick Booraem's involvement in golf lessened during the twenties. In the late thirties Hendrick and Mary Booraem moved to Florida, and on to Atlanta. Hendrick Booraem eventually returned to Minneapolis and died there in 1951 at the age of 66.

The Club quickly tapped into the pent-up demand for another Minneapolis golf club, swelling its membership ranks to 127 by August 1, 1916. The first payment was made on the land, and with the advice and guidance of Interlachen head pro George Sargent, the members cleared enough trees and brush north of the railroad tracks to lay out a crude nine-hole course less than a month after the Club was incorporated. There were farm houses, barns and other out buildings on the property, including a cluster to the left of the first fairway, two hundred yards from the current tee. The four-room Varner farmhouse, located near the present twelfth green, was remodeled as a temporary clubhouse, with members donating the furnishings. Victor Larson was hired as greenkeeper.

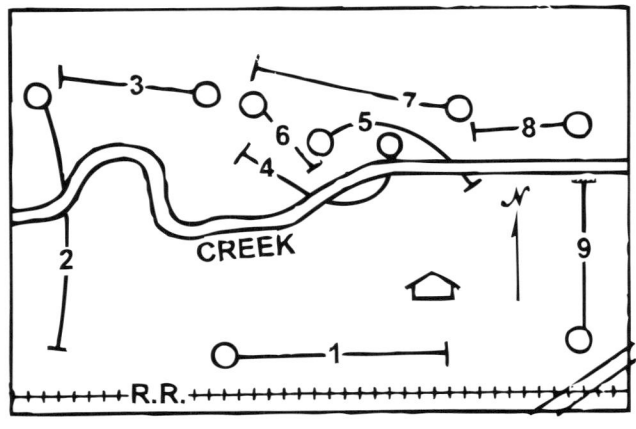

First Nine Holes 1915
Courtesy: GVGCC

The August 4, 1916 Minneapolis Morning Tribune announced: "New Local Golf Club to Open Course Saturday." The story reported that The Minneapolis Golf Club would "formally open its temporary nine-hole course tomorrow with a program of exercises and golf stunts."

Founding member Walter Fleck described the day as "delightful." That Saturday at 12:30 in the afternoon, a convoy of automobiles carried members to the course from Hennepin Avenue and Fifth Street. A buffet luncheon was served, followed by a Grand March to the first tee, led by Spark Plug, the horse the Club had rescued from the Humane Society to help with course maintenance.

"Spark Plug had been curried and powdered, his tail and mane braided with pink ribbons, and Eugene Bibb was selected to ride him," Fleck recalled 34 years later. "With his golf clubs on his back and a paper hat, he looked quite like a knight of old. Members of the Club followed on foot. Alas for Eugene Bibb, Spark Plug became excited and threw him off." The Grand March concluded with a driving contest. Then the Club officers teed off in a foursome, followed by additional foursomes of members.

Three photos taken at the Minneapolis Golf Club opening ran in the August 13 Minneapolis Morning Tribune, with the accompanying caption: "The links at present are rather undeveloped, but the topography of the land owned by the club gives ideal facilities for a first-class course."

The intent of the Club was to use the temporary 1,875-yard nine-hole course for the rest of the season, and build a new eighteen-hole course the following spring, along with a fitting clubhouse. There were also plans for a nine-hole course for women. Elwood Queen, assistant to George Sargent at Interlachen, was hired as the Club's first head pro, and prominent golf course architect Tom Bendelow of Chicago was summoned to design the permanent course. "The present course, though short, is difficult, because of the many natural hazards," the Morning Tribune reported. "The natural hazards are mostly in the form of bogs, trees almost in the fairways and Bassett's [sic] creek, which runs through the grounds."

Tom Bendelow with Early Advertisement
Courtesy: Stuart Bendelow

Tom Bendelow

Tom Bendelow
Courtesy: Stuart Bendelow

Tom Bendelow was America's first prolific golf course architect, and though much of his work from the early part of the twentieth century has been renovated or remodeled, he had a reputation for producing quality as well as quantity. Bendelow's first work in Minnesota was in 1908, when he was hired to refine the Minikahda Club course. He redesigned the original nine-hole Lafayette Club course in 1915 and designed the Minnetonka Country Club course in 1916. He was later hired to create the original 18-hole course at Edina Country Club. Prior to his visit to Golden Valley in September 1916, the Minneapolis Morning Tribune referred to Bendelow and Donald Ross as "the two best-known golf course architects in the United States."

Bendelow was born in Aberdeen, Scotland in 1868, and had played most of the significant courses in Scotland and England before moving to the United States in 1892. He played an exhibition match with English champion Harry Vardon in 1900. A deeply religious man, Bendelow never drank, never cursed and never played golf on Sunday. His one vice was smoking cigars.

While working in the composing room of the New York Herald, Bendelow answered a classified ad that led to his teaching golf to the family of Charles Pratt, co-founder of Standard Oil. He laid out a short golf course on the Pratt estate on Long Island – the first of hundreds he would design.

In 1895, he was hired by the A.G. Spalding Company to develop golf courses in the New York/New Jersey area. He gradually gave up his newspaper work, and in 1898 he was hired by the city of New York to redesign Van Cortlandt Park, which became the first eighteen-hole public golf course in the country. Bendelow subsequently moved to Chicago as Spalding's Golf Department manager. He spent the next twenty years traveling the country, often by automobile, to promote golf and design golf courses. By the time Bendelow came to Golden Valley, he was already credited with laying out more than 700 golf courses in the United States and Canada, and his methods had become more sophisticated over the course of his career. Although much of his early work was referred to as Eighteen Stakes on a Sunday Afternoon, he was one of the first golf architects to create elaborately detailed plans and mold plaster scale models of golf holes.

Bendelow's most recognizable surviving design is Medinah #3 in Chicago, site of three U.S. Opens, two PGA championships and the 2012 Ryder Cup. Tom Bendelow died in River Forest, Illinois, in 1936.

When Bendelow arrived at Golden Valley on Monday, August 28, 1916, he seemed not to notice, or be too concerned about, the bogs, trees and creek. As is the penchant of golf course architects to this day, Bendelow praised the property as being ideal for golf. He told the Morning Tribune that the new Minneapolis Golf Club would have one of the finest and most complete golf courses in the Northwest. Bendelow laid out an eighteen-hole course with a total distance of 6,685 yards, "which would make it the longest in this section." He completely disregarded the existing nine holes.

"The topography and soil conditions here are by far, the most ideal that I have found in years," Bendelow said. "The ground is all of the rolling meadow variety and can be converted into links easily. The soil is heavy loam and will not bake hard with the hot drought. I have mapped out a course which will have no parallel fairways and which will be almost perfect in every respect."

Bendelow returned Tuesday to make minor tweaks to his design, with the idea that construction work could begin Wednesday. Because of the late time of year, Bendelow suggested that the Club put a large crew of men on the job.

"Practically every inch of the land will be plowed and seeded before cold weather," the Tribune reported. "Also the putting greens will be worked over and seeded. It is declared that by planting the grass seed now it will mature with the very first days of spring and Mr. Bendelow stated that by July next year the new course will be in condition for play. Until then the temporary course will be used. In some places where the course conflicts, arrangements will be made for the play to continue.

"The plan for a special nine-hole course for women was abandoned by the Club officials yesterday on the advice of Mr. Bendelow, who said that special tees could be placed for women on the larger course, which would be much more satisfactory."

Bendelow did not sketch in many artificial hazards, believing the presence of Bassett Creek, the railroad tracks, roads, hills and trees would make "sufficient trouble" for the players. Before leaving town on Friday, September 1, Bendelow laid out a 2,200-yard 9-hole course for the Minnetonka Country Club, and then caught a train for another assignment in El Paso, Texas.

Work commenced on the new course in mid-September, but came to a sudden halt a month later. There would be a Minneapolis Golf Club, but it wasn't going to be in Golden Valley.

Original 16th Green
Courtesy: GVGCC

Chick Evans Has Greatest Chance of Taking Double Golf Honors

SPORTING SECTION
The Minneapolis Tribune

MINNEAPOLIS, MINN., SUNDAY, AUGUST 13, 1916.

Olga Dorfner Is After World's Swimming Marks

Miss Olga Dorfner

Philadelphia, Aug. 13.—(Special.)— Miss Olga Dorfner slipped back quietly into Philadelphia last week after taking the Pacific coast by storm with a series of brilliant swimming achievements.

"And now I'd like to equal the world's record," said Miss Dorfner. The Philadelphian has a handicap of two and three-fifths seconds to overcome before she equals the time established by the title holder, Fannie Durack, of Australia. The latter's time for 100 yards is 1:06.

It was just five weeks ago that Miss Dorfner left for the West, and during her absence she set a new American record for 100 yards and clipped two seconds from the time she previously established for the same distance.

Sets Records.

Under the auspices of the A. A. U. in California, Miss Dorfner met six of the fastest women contestants from this country and the Hawaiian Islands, and her amazing speed set the officials to checking up new figures for women—1:06 3-5 for 100 yards. Later in Oakland, Cal., the Philadelphia girl won a special 100-yard race from a former rival, Miss Claire Galligan of New York, in 1:11 2-5, which broke a record she previously established for the Schuylkill event of 1:14.

Miss Dorfner's latest achievement entitles her to a gold medal awarded by the A. A. U. This swells a notable list of trophies which she gained on previous occasions, when she established records in 40-yard, 80-yard and 220-yard races. She also holds records for the quarter-mile, the half-mile and the plunge for distance. One of her most meritorious feats was the perfect mark of 100 with which she passed the examination of the life saving corps.

Miss Minneapolis Declared a Formidable Contender for Gold Cup at Detroit Races

Detroit, Mich., Aug. 13.—All records for fast water traveling are expected to be broken when the speediest power boats of the country meet in the fourteenth annual gold challenge cup championship races over the picturesque Detroit river course off Belle Isle, September 2, 4, 5, 6.

Speed boats, some of them with records of better than a mile a minute, hailing from all over the country, and each with its backers believing it capable of wresting the coveted cup from the Miss Detroit, the boat which brought the cup west for the first time last year, have already entered.

Miss Detroit Entered.

Miss Detroit, raced by the Miss Detroit Power Boat association, captured the cup at Manhasset bay, L. I., last year, and is being groomed by her backers to duplicate the performance on her home course this September. Detroit alone will have three entries to defend the cup which the Miss Detroit won at Manhasset Bay last fall. The new Baby Harold, which has not yet had her maiden dip in the water and which has been built for C. Harold Wills, the Miss Detroit and Miss Hamtramck are the Detroit hydroplanes that will attempt to keep the cup, despite the bids that will be made to lift it by half a dozen or more fast boats representing other cities.

Miss Minneapolis Fastest.

One of the most formidable contenders for the gold trophy is the Miss Minneapolis, which, during the interlake regatta at Put-in-Bay set a new world's record of 66.46 miles per hour. It was built by the C. C. Smith Boat and Engine company, as was the Miss Detroit, which won the race last fall, but in some eight miles per hour faster than the Miss Detroit, the fast time made by the gold cup winner being a fraction better than 58 miles.

The Wills boat is built along the same lines as the Miss Detroit but is larger and will have a big increase in horsepower, and be driven by a Van Blerck engine instead of a Sterling. It will have 650 horsepower.

Very little is known of the Miss Hantramck.

Hawkeye, the hydroplane owned by President A. L. Judson, of the American Power Boat association, will be one of the eastern boats to come. This boat burned at Manhassett Bay last year and has been rebuilt for another attempt to lift the trophy.

Amateurs in Merion Meet Next Month

Grantland Rice Points Out Evans Will Have Fine Field to Beat.

LUCK OF GAME ALWAYS TO BE CONSIDERED, TOO

But Chick Is Last of Big Trio With Shot at Double Title.

By GRANTLAND RICE

Has the year finally arrived when America is to present a golfer capable of winning both the open championship and the amateur championship the same season?

Merion, Penn., will answer this query in September.

Exactly 26 years ago John Ball proved that the trick of winning the leading medal and match play competitions could be turned. Ball that year won both the British amateur and the British open, to the great astonishment of the golf world, who had no idea such an achievement could be put through. Two years later Harold Hilton achieved the same eminent destiny. But so far the United States of America has had no one golfer to offer as a brilliant parallel to Ball and Hilton, the two English stars.

The Third Chance.

When Evans goes to Merion in September he will be the last of the great trio to have a clean shot at the double title.

In 1913 Ouimet won the open but he had lost to Travers in the amateur.

Last year Travers won the open but Max Marston eliminated Jerry at Detroit by playing the last 12 holes in 43 strokes, five under 4s and three under par. Travers just had started coming to the top of his game when Marston struck his unbeatable whirl of play, as Jerry's chance to win both events the same year faded on the 25th green. And the tough part of it all was that Jerry went down after playing the last 14 holes exactly in par, neither one stroke better nor one stroke worse than par on any one of these holes.

Up to Evans.

Where Travers back in the early days and where Ouimet and Travers of later seasons failed, Evans still has his chance. Ouimet won the open in 1913 and the amateur in 1914, but he was unable to buck both together the same year.

Now enters Chick, the last of the Three Musketeers of American golf, to take his shot at the double pointed heights.

This Merion affair will be a harder test for Chick than the open was. In the first place Evans has always been rated better at medal play, largely because he has putted with greater consistency in the former test.

Then, in match play, no matter how fine a golfer a man may be, one day's lapse will drop him out. Or, if he doesn't run into a lapse, there is a telling jolt when he will run against some golfer shooting his bally head off in an exceptional round.

Last year, for example, at Detroit, any number of golfers were able to keep well in the lead playing from 78 to 81. Yet against Sawyer in the forenoon Evans had a 74 was 5 down! He had merely happened to run against an opponent playing the best golf of the tournament that day.

The Smashing Test.

A U. S. G. A. championship now at match play has gotten to be a smashing test. In addition to Evans, there are Jerry Travers, Bob Gardner, Oswald Kirkby, Max Marston, New Sawyer, Reggie Lewis and several others who are likely to travel around in 72 or 73. There are at least a dozen amateurs now who may beat 76 at any given round.

And these no longer falter before champions. That was proved at Detroit when Evans, Travers and Ouimet all of them in fine physical shape or he might not be able to bear up under the heavy strain. To move from one touch opponent to another and to know that any one round may bring defeat does not leave much of a breathing spell. It is certainly no place for a golfer who starts in stale. The best chance belongs to the entry who is just coming on to his game as the tournament opens and who is thereby picking up more and more confidence with each round.

The man who goes through the amateur championship at Merion must first of all be in fine physical shape or he might not be able to bear up under the heavy strain. To move from one touch opponent to another and to know that any one round may bring defeat does not leave much of a breathing spell. It is certainly no place for a golfer who starts in stale. The best chance belongs to the entry who is just coming on to his game as the tournament opens and who is thereby picking up more and more confidence with each round.

At the Opening of the Minneapolis Golf Club

PUTTING on the EIGHTH GREEN

R. O. JOHNSON, VICE PRESIDENT, READING the TEN COMMANDMENTS of GOLF

HENDRICK BOORAEM, PRESIDENT

The Minneapolis Golf club, which formally opened its course at Golden Valley last Sunday, is the newest golfing organization in the city, really making five clubs for Minneapolis. A nine-hole course has been laid out for this summer and next spring it will be increased to 18 holes. The links at present are rather undeveloped, but the topography of the land owned by the club gives ideal facilities for a first-class course.

mined an 18-inch putt. These incidents go to show just what happens in a championship tournament where there is very little difference among the leading 10.

The Luck of the Draw.

There is a lot, too, in the luck of the draw. To win a championship, the victor must win five 36-hole matches. Suppose it fell to Evans' lot to meet Travers, Kirkby, Marston and Gardner in order. He might beat any one or any two of these. But beating all four in succession would be well-nigh hopeless.

Then again there is the proposition of going against an opponent who looks to be easy and have said opponent romp around in 74 or 75. In the recent New Jersey championship Oswald Kirkby drew Henry Seggerman for his first opponent.

Kirkby had been giving Seggerman three strokes without any trouble. Yet in this match Kirkby was around in 73 and still Seggerman had only to make a three-foot putt to win on the 18th green. If that three-footer had dropped, Kirkby, despite his fine golf, would have been beaten in his first round without ever drawing the chance to overthrow Max Marston in the 36-hole final.

Training for a Championship.

Apparently the best way to train for a championship is not to take it too seriously.

In 1912 Ouimet had no idea of playing at Brookline until Robert C. Watson made him enter. Even then Francis entered merely for the experience and for something of a lark. But he nearly won from Vardon and Ray.

In 1916 Evans says he was playing ankle before the open and then decided to enter for the fun of it. Walter Hagen beat him by only one stroke for the title.

In 1915 Travers had been playing very little golf. He had no idea of entering two weeks before the tournament. He finally decided to play for the recreation without any thought of success. Four days later he was open champion.

In 1916 Evans says he was playing the worst golf of many months before the tournament started. He first decided not to go. Then he decided later to take a week's vacation just to be around. A week before the tournament he wasn't even certain that he could qualify. But he went for the recreation again and today is open champion.

Rod and Reel — By Dixie Carroll

HOT WEATHER FISHING.

My Dear Buck:

When the days are hot and the old king of coldwater is lying on the bottom, it is doing his best for the cure and his worst for the fisherman, it takes our entire deck of tricks to lure the game fish out of the deep, cool holes. Mid-summer heat drives the fish down to great depth in search of cold water and during only a few hours in the very early morning and at night they come into the shallows to feed. At that time casting will land 'em, the rest of the day you simply have to go down for them or sit on the cabin porch and hold a talkfest on how you landed that "big 'un" a couple years ago.

Send the Bait Down.

For the hot weather, the greatest little old coaster is live bait. Among the most used live ones are the minnows, worms, helgramite, crawfish and frogs, while the grasshopper if used as a surface bait on streams will get a rise out of a big trout of bass, when he wouldn't even take a look at a fly.

If you are after bass, old man, when the mercury is popping high, locate a sand-bar or spring hole anywhere from 30 to a 100 feet down, if your fishing waters go that deep, let your little old live bait slowly settle to them and you will get bass when the other fellow finds it necessary to be satisfied with pan fish. Right in mid-season when the mercury was flirting with the 90 degree mark on an afternoon I have had plenty of sport still-fishing for small-mouth bass. On Black lake in northern Wisconsin, with Earny Wendt, the truest little old guide that ever handled a paddle, we had located a school of small-mouth and by sending our soul minnows down to them, depleted the school to such an extent that the old "be now" teacher closed up for want of scholars. The water is exceptionally clear in Black lake and at from 30 to 40 feet, Earny, with his eagle eyes, could locate a school of bass and we would quietly fish it to a fare-you-well. From our school of 11 fine fellows we took right before they wised up to the fact that there was a string to the bait offer. Often three or four bass would make a dart for the minnow only to be disappointed by the winner swimming off with his prey to stop and swallow it at his leisure. The run of the bass in this school, before stopping to swallow the bait varied from 40 to 90 feet.

Sport Fit for a King.

A few seasons ago at a lake that is considered very civilized waters and which has been fished to a finish for the past 20 years, three fishermen landed as nice a bunch of small-mouth bass on a hot August day as ever falls to the lot of an angler, and at that generally in his dreams. With a sun that burned through their shirts, these knights of the rod stuck to a spring hole they had located down from 90 feet of water, caught 48 small-mouth bass, 10 of which ranged from three and a half pounds. And the bait they used was the common, wiggling angleworm. That same day many fishermen were casting in the shallows and failed to bring in enough bass to make a fair-sized breakfast.

Big Ones Were There.

The wall-eyed pike is by nature a bottom fish and any part of the season you have to go down for him, although at night he often comes into the shallows to feed. The usual thing is to troll for them in from 15 to 30 feet of water. I have always had an idea, old-timer, that in deep lakes you could find him in warm weather in deeper water. I tried it out and sure enough I found him there. I trolled over a piece of near shore water with a depth of about 15 feet and the average wall-eye caught ranged from one and a half to two pounds. I then rigged up a regular deepwater trolling rig generally used for lake trout and the first strike was a six-pounder. I trolled back and forth over this stretch of water and landed seven wall-eyed ranging from three and a quarter to seven and a half pounds. The average depth of the water was about 50 feet; it varied between 30 and 65 feet.

How to Make the Rig.

The rig for this deep trolling is easily assembled and is sure takes your bait down to them. Take an eight-ounce, cone-shaped sinker and attach it to the end of your line with a swivel, then take three pieces of line about three feet long and attach the first piece with a swivel to the line about three feet above the sinker. Three feet above the first line attach the second with a swivel and three feet above that attach the other with a swivel. On the three ends of these lines swivel on an eight-inch piano wire leader, because the big wall-eyed pike have teeth that will cut through a line or gut leader. To your leaders attach either a single hook or a treble as you prefer; on each of these hooks bait with a six to eight-inch shiner or golden club. Let your line down and find bottom, then troll along very slowly. The wall-eyed will strike very mildly for his size and swim away slowly with the bait. Let him take it some distance, then strike him and if he is any size you will have a fine time bringing him up to the boat. Fact is he will probably make a couple of runs back to the bottom just when you think you have him to net. With this rig I had the fun of landing ten wall-eyed pike at once, a three and three-quarter pounder and a five and a quarter and you can take it for mine, old-timer, I know there was something on the line when they both began to "act up" for company. In making this rig I think that you will have tackle by using a double piece of line for your sinker connection than your reel line, as the sinker is liable to catch in the rocks on the bottom, and if the connecting line is weaker it will break and you only lose the sinker. A small spoon, say about a No. 3, placed in front of the bait will make it more attractive, or an Archer spinner ought to look good to most wall-eye.

—DIXIE

Sunday Is a Hoodoo Day for the Cleveland Team; July Percentage Just 250

The Indians started off grandly this year in their Sunday combats, and for quite a time were known as the Sabbath champions. To move from one touch day has been a day of misfortune for them.

On the last Sunday in May the Dunnmen were twice shut out by the Sox and on the third Sunday in June the Yankee's murdered Fohl's charges, 19 to 3.

Cleveland's Sunday percentage for July was just .250. On July 2 St. Louis was beaten, but on July 16 Washington triumphed. The Browns, on July 23, downed the Cleveland pennant entry, 5 to 2. That game went into overtime. Ten innings were played July 30 and Cleveland lost again.

The worst thing that happened to the Indians on a Sunday this year was Speaker's injury on the Sabbath day.

DON'T CHEER TOO SOON.

Baseball and life are the same in a way.

They are crowded with gladness and sadness.

For a ball team will play like a winner today.

And a minor league bunch on the morrow.

Showing Some Speed — By Wheelan

The August 13, 1916 Minneapolis Morning Tribune gave top billing to the opening of the original golf course, first known as Minneapolis Golf Club

Courtesy: Minneapolis Morning Tribune

PART TWO ~

LEFT BEHIND

A three-paragraph story in the October 27 *Minneapolis Morning Tribune* reported the basics:

> ### GOLF CLUB CHANGES SITE
>
> The Minneapolis Golf Club has decided to abandon its property at Golden Valley and has purchased a 500-acre tract of land at Richmond, one and a half miles the other side of St. Louis Park, between the Minnetonka and Superior boulevards.
>
> Willie Parks [sic], a New York golf architect, has been over the property and declared it suitable for golfing purposes. He will lay out an 18-hole course soon.
>
> The Golden Valley site was given up because of its inaccessibility. Only an option had been obtained for its purchase.

There was more to the story than that, however. Walter Fleck, one of Minneapolis Golf Club's seven founding members, recalled the circumstances of the location switch in a memoir written for the program of the U.S. Amateur Championship, held at Minneapolis Golf Club in 1950:

"The [Minneapolis Golf] Club was offered our present site by the Hylands Home company, who intended to organize a golf club there. This course was being laid out by Willie Parks [actually Park], famous Scotch golf champion and noted golf-course architect. This prospective golf course had much better possibilities than the course we had laid out and started to use. The price per acre was less, the same payable on twenty-year bonds at 5½ percent. We were also given a loan of $45,000 to build the eighteen holes and reconstruct a farmhouse on the grounds into a clubhouse, located where our fifteenth tee is now. A committee was appointed to consider the proposition and submit it with their recommendations to the Club. The proposition seemed most attractive, we were allowed to choose the ground we needed, out of several hundred acres available, containing the two water-holes and no roads cutting through the course. The tract of land we chose was about one hundred and forty acres. The proposition, being acceptable to the committee, was submitted to the membership at a special meeting, and a vote of acceptance received from the members."

Original 11th Hole
Courtesy: GVGCC

With that, a majority of the members of the brand-new Minneapolis Golf Club abandoned the Golden Valley site for St. Louis Park, leaving forty members behind who preferred their original location.

Those remaining forty decided to press on, hoping there was enough demand for two new golf clubs in the western suburbs of Minneapolis, and the new Golden Valley Golf Club was incorporated on December 21, 1916. Regular members were required to be stockholders of the corporation, adult male residents of Minnesota and be nominated and elected by other members. Of the corporation's original $50,000 in capital stock, $40,000 was preferred stock and the remaining $10,000 was common stock. No shareholder was entitled to more than one vote, or more than one share of common stock. The Club set a debt limit of $250,000, to be used strictly for developing a golf course and building a clubhouse. The initiation fee was doubled to fifty dollars for the next sixty new members, after which the fee would double again to one hundred dollars.

A discrepancy exists over who became president of the Golden Valley Golf Club at that point. In a 1943 synopsis of the Club's history, Arthur Statt wrote that Milton Huber was the newly incorporated Club's first president, followed by Hendrick Booraem. Yet newspaper accounts of the Club's affairs in 1917 consistently refer to Booraem as Golden Valley's president, with Huber serving as secretary.

The January 20, 1917, *Minneapolis Morning Tribune* reported that a meeting was held at the West Hotel for the purpose of launching a campaign to increase the membership to two hundred before May 1. "Every one of the members present promised to secure at least one additional member before February 9, when another meeting will be called and when the campaign will be formally organized with two teams competing to secure members," the story said. "Plans of the Club were outlined by Hendrik Booraem, president, John Pears, treasurer, and Harry W. Miller, vice president, who is also acting as the chairman of the membership committee.

"Mr. Pears told of the financial condition of the Club. He declared that with 60 additional members, making 100 in all, the Club will be assured of the completion of the first nine holes, while the 200 would make it possible to complete the full 18. The membership limit is set at 400, but only half that number is the present goal."

With its decimated membership, the entire focus was put on getting the golf course built – "a purely playing club with the social side subordinated in order to make the running as economical as possible," the paper reported. The temporary clubhouse would remain in use for the foreseeable future. It was also announced that Bendelow would return to Golden Valley in the spring to rearrange some of the holes, primarily to eliminate several forced carries across the railroad tracks.

In March of 1917, the Club hired Englishman Walter Andrews as head golf professional. Elwood Queen had gone with most of the original members to the new site in St. Louis Park, and then accepted a job as assistant at his former Club in Chevy Chase, Maryland. Andrews had been at the Bloomington (Illinois) Country Club for the previous three years. He came to the United States in 1912 from the Royal North Devon Golf Club, where he was an apprentice to noted golf instructor Charles Gibson. In March, Bendelow completed his revised plan for the eighteen-hole course, changing the layout so that no holes crossed the railroad tracks.

A Walter Andrews Golf Club
Courtesy: Joe Gladke

The new plan reduced the proposed length of the course to 6,340 yards. "Work will be started just as soon as the snow goes away," the Tribune reported. "The nine-hole course will be lengthened to nearly 3,000 yards for temporary play."

When Andrews arrived in April, he was greeted by a problem that would persist at Golden Valley for a number of years: Bassett Creek ("on its annual rampage," according to the Tribune), had flooded the course's low ground, and washed out the bridge between the eighth and ninth holes. Nevertheless, twenty-five members played on the nine-hole course on April 7, skipping the soggy holes. Andrews laid out three new holes on the south side of the railroad tracks to add to the first six holes of the temporary course.

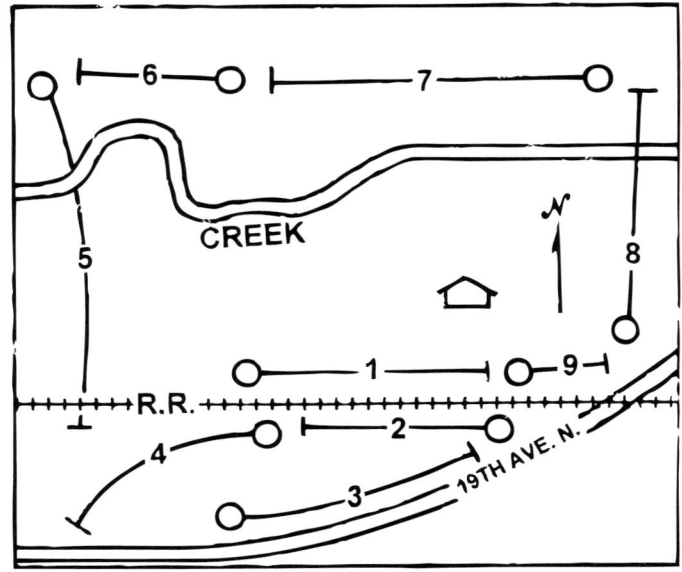

Second Nine Holes 1917
Courtesy: GVGCC

By the end of April, the Club was nearing its goal of one hundred total members, though it had decided to reduce the initiation fee to seventy-five dollars, rather than one hundred dollars, for those joining after the century mark was reached.

World War I was becoming an issue for golf clubs; Golden Valley announced that Club members who entered military service would not be asked to pay dues while they were away. In addition, Andrews announced that Golden Valley would join with the other city golf clubs and use a part of the course for growing vegetables as a war measure. Four acres of potatoes were planted in the corners of the fairways.

The 1917 golf season officially opened on a cold, wet Saturday, April 28, starting with a luncheon at the temporary clubhouse, where a row of small wooden lockers and a single shower had been installed. A shed had been constructed behind the converted farm house to serve as a bar room, with sawdust spread on the clay floor. President Booraem discussed plans for the coming season, and the members played a low medal and blind bogey event. Milton Huber and C.E. Overshire tied for the low net round of 42, while William Cavan had the low medal score of 43. Andrews had lengthened the temporary nine-hole course considerably since his arrival, and it now played 3,300 yards long.

The Club typically had 60 players or more on the course during that first full season, and a new game was introduced to accommodate the large numbers. Called a "gangsome" (a version of what is now called a shootout), the entire company of players teed off at the same tee, immediately following one another. No player left the tee until each one had driven. At the first hole, the players failing to hole out within the strokes determined beforehand were eliminated, and the game continued until only two were left, at which point it became match play. In the meantime, the eliminated players started back at the first tee to continue their round.

As was common practice in the early years of golf, the Club put together a team of about twenty players to challenge teams from other courses. On June 3 the Golden Valley team, captained by Booraem, hosted the team from the new Glenwood public golf course. Later that summer, the Golden Valley team played a home-and-home series against the team from the Red Wing Country Club, and visited the Minnetonka Country Club as well. There were also internal matches for season-long Club honors. Booraem defeated Charles Sawyer (father of future Golden Valley whiz kid Pat Sawyer) in a semi-final match for the Director Trophy, and faced Ed Longley in the finals (there is no record available of who won the match). Longley, a former runner-up in the Trans-Mississippi Tournament, set the amateur course record in May with a 73; Andrews held the overall record at 71.

In addition to Longley, the best player that first summer at Golden Valley Golf Club was Earl Judkins, head of the Club's sports and pastimes committee, who reached the semi-finals of the State Amateur in 1918 and the quarterfinals the following year. Judkins was the first club champion at Glenwood Golf Course and the Golden Valley club champion in 1918 as well.

In the meantime, work progressed slowly on building the promised Tom Bendelow eighteen-hole course. The August 17 Morning Tribune reported that Andrews had just completed several additions to the first nine holes, now measuring 2,535 yards: "The No. 3 hole has been lengthened 60 yards, making the hole 310 yards long now. The hole is now a good drive carry over the creek and a mashie [5-iron] shot. The new distance takes away much of the advantage poorer players had on the hole who usually made their plan of attack two shorter iron shots. No. 6 has been lengthened 50 yards and the tee at the ninth hole has been set back so that the hole now requires a good drive and mashie additional. The hole distance is now 350 yards. Work will start on the second

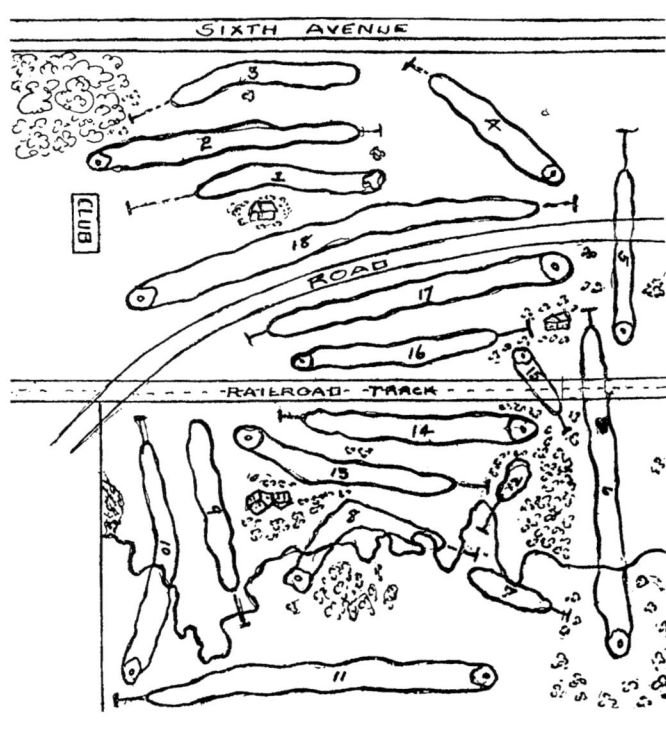

Original Bendelow 1917 Layout
Courtesy: Minneapolis Morning Tribune

nine holes of the Golden Valley course within a month and the full route will be in use for the early play next spring."

In September, the paper reported that Andrews had been authorized by the directors to begin working on the second nine holes of Bendelow's plan. The architect returned to the Club in October to alter his original design, telling the Club's Board the contour of the land and its beauty, in time, would make it equal to any course in the state. He called one of his holes, the 350-yard dogleg-left eighth hole, one of the "sportiest" he had ever designed, requiring the drive and the approach shot to cross the creek a total of four times. Cost of the course, which was projected to open in May 1918, would run $25,000.

Andrews would not be around to see the new course, however. In late October, it was announced that Otis George, who had been the head professional at the Lafayette Club for the previous six years, would become the pro at Golden Valley Golf Club in 1918. Construction had already begun on the full Bendelow design; fifty men and eight teams of horses were busy building the new holes under the direction of J.A. Stafford, Bendelow's superintendent of construction. When George returned in April from spending the winter at the Kissimmee Golf Club in Florida (a club whose course he built in 1914), he assumed upkeep of the new course in addition to his professional duties. There was a concern, however; George was subject to the draft, with no claim to a deferral. In February he was called to take a physical.

Meanwhile, at the Club's annual meeting in December, John Burgess was elected the new president, and dues were raised from thirty dollars to forty dollars.

George arrived in Minneapolis on March 19, 1918, to assume his new duties. He inspected the temporary nine hole course and announced that seven of the holes would be ready to play by the end of the week. The other two, typically, were under water.

The condition of the golf course soon became an afterthought, however; in the early morning of April 7, the Golden Valley clubhouse burned down. The old farmhouse had recently benefited from a

Original 6th Hole
Courtesy: GVGCC

refurbishing, with a locker room and showers added to the west side of the house. A strong wind caused the blaze to spread so rapidly that the structure was a total loss by the time fire crews arrived. Members who showed up that day to play golf were dismayed to see the charred and smoldering remains of the building. Officials placed the value of the structure at $7,000, only partially covered by insurance.

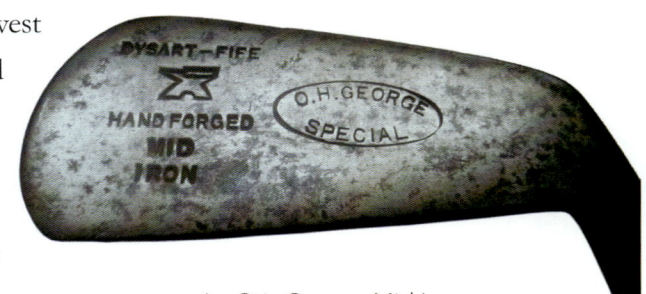

An Otis George Mid Iron
Courtesy: Joe Gladke

The executive committee held an all-day session and came up with plans for member William Tell to immediately build another clubhouse. The committee said the new building would be bigger and better in every way than the old one, and would include a club room, ladies room, grill room and showers. It was expected to be completed in three or four weeks. In the interim, the other two buildings owned by the Club would serve as temporary shelters, "and all the comforts of the old structure will be afforded the golfers."

The 1918 golf season had already begun with plenty of excitement, and it continued when Lafayette pro Harry Van Every – a scratch player, and the uncle of future Golden Valley legend Harold Van Every – shot a 69 in a sweepstakes event on April 13. Former Chicago amateur Andy Martin lowered that record to 66 in May, and in June Otis George shot a 63 in a casual round. A few hours later he went back out and shot a 67 in an amateur-professional match.

George's stint as Golden Valley pro came to an abrupt halt later that June. He and Van Every were both drafted and ordered to report to Camp Grant, the U.S. Army training base outside Rockford, Illinois. George's place was taken by his assistant, John Dryburgh, who followed George from Lafayette.

By July 1918, two-thirds of the permanent new course was open, and using six holes from the original nine, the Club was finally playing an eighteen-hole course. Earl Judkins wasted no time setting the course record with a 74 on the first day of play. On July 11, Dryburgh topped that with a 73. Later that summer Bill Barrett, assistant pro at Interlachen, would lower the record to 70. Citing the impact of the war, however, the Club did not have enough money to finish the course that year.

In December, the Club announced that Cyril Walker of Westfield, New Jersey, would be the new head pro for 1919, replacing Dryburgh, who took a head pro job in Aberdeen, South Dakota. Walker, an Englishman who was recommended by George Sargent of Interlachen, was considered an excellent builder of golf courses, and was put in charge of adding the finishing touches to Golden Valley's eighteen-hole layout.

After electing Jean Hartzell as new Club president, the predominant issue for the membership, now numbering 242, was how to raise the $15,000 - 20,000 needed to complete and improve the 18-hole course.

Bassett Creek often flooded holes such as the original Bendelow 16th
Courtesy: GVGCC

Cyril Walker

Born in Manchester, England, on September 18, 1892, Walker immigrated to the United States in 1914 and took a job as the first golf pro at Shackamaxon Country Club in Scotch Plains, New Jersey. He began winning U.S. tournaments in 1916 and was one of the nation's best players by the time he served his one season as Golden Valley's head professional in 1919.

Walker was the club pro at Englewood Golf Club in New Jersey when he entered the 1924 U.S. Open at Oakland Hills Country Club outside Detroit. Bobby Jones was the defending champion and prohibitive favorite; Walker had finished 13th, 40th and 23rd in the previous three Opens. At Oakland Hills, Walker was tied for the lead with Jones through three rounds, and Jones took leader in the clubhouse with a final-round 78. Walker then came in with a 75, the second-best score of the day, to beat Jones by three shots. At 118 pounds,

Cyril Walker
Courtesy: USGA

Walker was the Open's second-lightest champion after Fred McLeod, who weighed only 108 pounds at the time of his victory in the 1908 U.S. Open.

As his career progressed, Walker developed a reputation for being an extremely slow player. During the second round of the 1930 Los Angeles Open, rules officials warned him for slow play at the sixth hole, to which he replied, "You won't disqualify me! I'm Cyril Walker, a former U.S. Open champion! I've come 5,000 miles to play in your diddy-bump tournament and I'll play as slow as I damn well please!" Walker was disqualified, but continued to play. Officials called police and had the furious Walker dragged off the course. Many pros declined to play with Walker after the incident, forcing tournament officials to send him out alone. His troubles increased as his drinking got out of hand; eventually he was found by a reporter working as a caddie at a municipal course in Miami Beach in 1940, looking far older than his 48 years and wearing a torn maroon turtle-neck sweater even on the hottest days because he didn't own a shirt.

On the night of April 5, 1948, Walker went to a police station in Hackensack, New Jersey, and asked the desk sergeant if he could sleep in a cell, because he didn't have a dime for lodging. He was given a cell, but when the sergeant went to wake him in the morning, he found Walker dead, slumped in a chair. He was fifty-six.

"In the early years before being properly drained, water stood in pools quite a while after a rain, and the turf and ground beneath was very soft," recalled longtime member Strowbridge Seaton. "Many a golf ball driven out on this soft turf would break through and be entirely buried out of sight and lost. Golfers tried to shoot to the higher ground around the edge of the fairway, but if they failed to do so and landed on soft turf, it meant a lost ball."

Seaton related that one of the Club's Board members was obsessed with finding a way to properly drain the lowest parts of the course. One day the Board member was in downtown Minneapolis and came across a workman carrying a ditching spade. Inspired, the Board member brought the workman and his spade out to Golden Valley, where he instructed the man to dig a twelve-inch wide ditch through part of the seventh fairway. By that evening, water was draining off the fairway through the ditch.

"After this proof of what could be done, work was started to remedy the wet condition of this fairway," Seaton wrote. Bassett Creek was dredged, straightened and dammed, forming a reservoir from which water was pumped into a pressure tank connected to pipes that delivered water all over the course.

In April 1919, Golden Valley Golf Club topped the 300-member mark. To make the Club more accessible and comfortable, the Board voted to purchase a bus to pick up members in downtown Minneapolis. They also agreed to extend the front porch across the full length of the clubhouse. On June 7, the Morning Tribune announced that Golden Valley's new course would open that afternoon.

"Construction ... has been in progress for several months," the paper reported. "It was pronounced ready for play yesterday by the club professional, Cyril Walker. Water connections have been completed and the course, with a total yardage of 6,382, is expected to provide some brand new problems for students of the drive and approach at the club. All permanent greens are ready with the exception of two. They will be in shape for putting within two weeks … The turf is in great condition and the course well supplied with bunkers and hazards that make it a real test of golf." Six holes were now located south of 19th Ave. North (now Golden Valley Road).

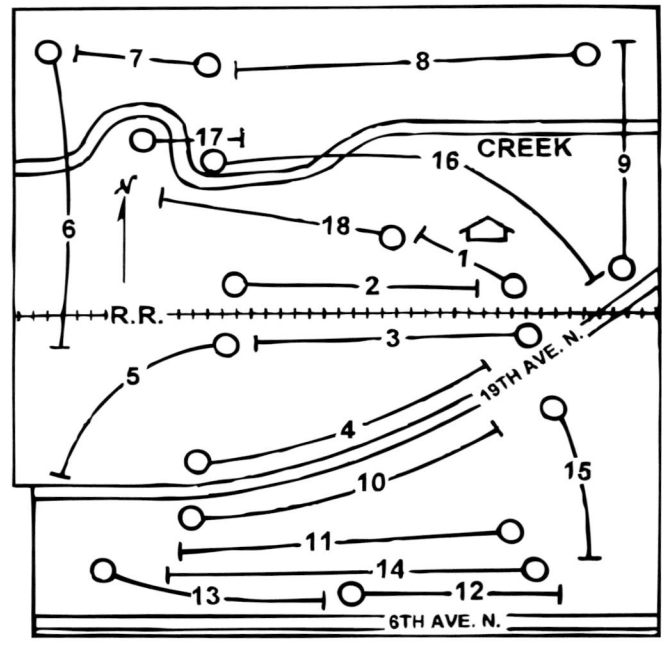

First Eighteen Holes 1919
Courtesy: GVGCC

With the war in Europe coming to an end, both Otis George and Harry Van Every were mustered out of the Army and returned to the Twin Cities. Van Every applied for and received reinstatement as an amateur, and went into the grain business. He also resumed his outstanding golf career, firing a 75 the morning of August 31 and a 74 that afternoon to defeat Al Collins 3 & 2 in a 36-hole match to become the new Club Champion at Golden Valley.

Needing a job, Otis George signed on as an assistant to Minneapolis Golf Club head pro Bill Clark, but when Cyril Walker told Golden Valley Golf Club that he was not going to return in 1920, the Club brought the popular George back as its head pro.

In March of 1920, George returned, with Minneapolis native Eddie McElligott as his assistant. Almost immediately, it was determined that the golf course was still in need of improvement. This time the Club turned to William Watson, an architect with an exceptional reputation in Minnesota, having designed the first courses at Minikahda, Interlachen and White Bear Yacht Club. Though Donald Ross had been brought in at each course to consult, upgrade or even do a complete redesign, Watson had his fingerprints on the most highly-regarded projects in Minnesota golf.

On April 4, the Tribune reported that Watson was going to do "an extensive rearrangement" of the Golden Valley course. President Hartzell told the paper that the work would cost $15,000, would be started immediately, and was expected to take sixty days. Temporary greens would be used during construction.

The specific changes Watson made have not been documented, but it was ready for play by June, when Otis George and his brother Dow defeated Interlachen head pro Willie Kidd and his assistant Bill Barrett 3 & 1 in a best ball match at Golden Valley. Otis George set the course record of 69 that summer, and Harry Van Every set the amateur record with a 70.

Jean Hartzell retained the presidency for a second year in 1921, and he and John Pears were joined on the Executive Committee by Austen Cargill, a man who would become instrumental in the survival of the Club during the Depression. Arthur Statt, another man whose impact at the club would span decades, was named membership chair.

The Club was beginning to hit its stride at last. Club manager Cliff Miller's Wednesday night buffet dinners were becoming an institution; reservations were required days in advance for a chance to dine on the Club's outstanding food for $1.50 a plate. "In those early days, the Club was always in financial difficulties, but that worried no one," Statt wrote in 1943. "Shortly after the first World War, golf became very popular, and the 400 limit of members was soon reached, and for several years a waiting list was in effect."

Members congregated every Saturday night to dance to five-piece bands, while nearby farmers and Club staff would sit on the railroad embankment outside the clubhouse and listen to the music. The Club took advantage of its proximity to downtown Minneapolis to offer noon lunch service.

Statt became Club president in 1922. He was one of the Club's better golfers, having teamed with Van Every earlier that summer to defeat Minneapolis Golf Club aces Jake Wetherby and Allan Labatt in a team match. His and the Club's focus in 1922 would be to prepare the golf course for its biggest test to date: hosting the Minnesota State Amateur championship for the first time.

"With sufficient funds already raised, the committee in charge will make the necessary changes in the course as soon as the warm weather appears in the spring," the Tribune reported. "The fairways are to be improved, new tees to replace the present ones, and from fifty to sixty traps added to those already on the links."

In fact, the Club ended up building forty new bunkers prior to the State Amateur, and the course played as a par 74 – 36 on the front nine and 38 on the back. Golden Valley Golf Club was ready for its coming-out party. The course itself proved to be a rugged test, sending qualifying scores soaring, and identifying a true champion: Jimmy Johnston.

Following the triumph of its first State Amateur, Golden Valley hosted the Minnesota State Open for the first time in 1923. Head pro Jack Burke of the Town & Country Club shot even par 296, with a low tournament round of 70, to win the four-day championship. Interlachen's Willie Kidd was second at 303, while Golden Valley's Russ Collins was low amateur at 310, finishing tied for eighth.

1922 Minnesota State Amateur Championship

Since its inception in 1901, the Minnesota State Amateur championship had rotated between the state's oldest clubs, having been played six times at the Minikahda Club, five times at the Town & Country Club, three times at Northland Country Club, twice at Interlachen and once at White Bear Yacht Club. In 1922, the Golden Valley Golf Club was deemed worthy to be included in the state rota.

The new king of Minnesota amateur golf, Harrison R. "Jimmy" Johnston, was the favorite in 1922, having won his first state title the previous year. Among the prominent contenders were Golden Valley's own Russell Collins and Harry Van Every. During the first qualifying round, Johnston lowered the amateur record at Golden Valley to 70. Otherwise, the scores were not particularly good – perhaps understandable, as the state's premier event had never been played there before. Collins tied for second with a 76. Johnston followed that round with a 71, becoming medalist by an astonishing sixteen strokes over Collins and F.M. Warner of Interlachen.

Jimmy Johnston
Courtesy: GVGCC

Johnston cruised to the final match, where he faced Minneapolis Golf Club's Jake Wetherby, who had knocked off home-course favorite Collins 2 & 1 in the semis. The Minneapolis Tribune tried to inject some life into accounts of the final match, referring to Wetherby "fighting gamely all the way and at times shooting sensational golf." Yet his putting was shaky all day, and Johnston scored an easy 7 & 6 victory. A large gallery followed the thirty-six-hole final match – a throng that "was responsible for several partly missed shots by both boys, who were crowded at times by the spectators eager to watch the play," the Tribune reported.

"The 1922 tournament can be safely called one of the most successful in recent years," the Tribune reported. "While the field didn't have the class of recent years, the tournament experience was worth a world of good to the youngsters who will show up well in a year or two. It is regretted that the players who could have pushed Johnston could not enter."

Those players never did materialize. In the next three State Amateur championships, Johnston posted final-round victory margins of 11 & 10, 13 & 12 and 9 & 8. He would ultimately win seven straight state titles, and cap his remarkable decade by winning the 1929 U.S. Amateur at Pebble Beach.

According to longtime member Strowbridge Seaton's 1984 historical memoir, the Golden Valley clubhouse burned down again in 1923. With the Club membership at full capacity, the Board decided to build a larger and more modern clubhouse. Two locations were considered, with one faction advocating that the clubhouse be built on a hill south of 19th Avenue North, near the current clubhouse, while another faction favored a site farther up the hill to the south, in the woods behind what is now the second green. After a prolonged and heated disagreement, the lower location prevailed.

The Club raised $25,000 through the sale of preferred stock to the membership to finance the construction in 1924. The clubhouse had locker rooms and the golf shop on the lower level, and the dining room, kitchen, club rooms and porch room on the upper level. Members gained access to the upper level by way of a circular driveway on top of the hill, and crossed from the eighteenth green to the locker rooms on the lower level through a tunnel in the side of the hill. William Tell built the new structure, Paul Zuppke supervised the construction, and Austen Cargill designed the locker room. The Board also purchased ten additional acres east of the new clubhouse at a bargain price, land that was eventually turned into the Club's current practice area.

Moving the clubhouse to the south set a number of dominoes in motion. What had been the tenth hole was changed to the first hole, and the fifteenth hole, a par-three with its tee located east of the current second green and its green somewhere near the current swimming pool, was eliminated. But simply renumbering and rerouting some of the existing holes was not considered adequate to address the desire to have two nine-hole loops that began and returned to the location of the new clubhouse. Once again, a golf course architect was needed, and this time Golden Valley reached out to one of the industry's biggest names: A. W. Tillinghast.

Golden Valley Clubhouse circa 1924
Courtesy: GVGCC

Arrangement of Holes 1924
Courtesy: GVGCC

Tillinghast, who had already designed Baltusrol Upper and Lower, Winged Foot East and West, San Francisco Golf Club and Somerset Hills (New Jersey) Country Club, was a hot commodity who demanded and got top dollar for his designs. It is unlikely that Golden Valley would have had a chance to lure Tilly (as he was known to friends and associates) to the Twin Cities had his daughter Elsie not married Mayo Clinic physician Dr. Phillip Brown. The Tillinghasts often visited the Browns in Rochester, Minnesota, and during one such visit, Tillinghast agreed to completely redesign the nine-hole Rochester Golf Club course free of charge, turning it into an eighteen-hole layout. Otto Seitzel's green committee invited Tillinghast to come to Golden Valley, hoping he might be willing to take on a similar project for them. According to Arthur Statt, Tillinghast "immediately saw the possibilities of a truly great golf course" and accepted the job. Work began in 1926, and was completed three years later.

A.W. Tillinghast

A. W. Tillinghast
Courtesy: Tillinghast Association

Former USGA Executive Director Frank Hannigan once described A. W. Tillinghast as "a superb, not a good or very good, but a superb course architect. His courses, properly cared for, improve with age." It is the timelessness of his designs that makes Tillinghast one of a small handful of great designers of golf's Golden Age.

Albert Warren Tillinghast was born May 7, 1874, in Philadelphia, the only child of Lavinia Morall Davis and Benjamin Collins Tillinghast, who owned the successful B.C. Tillinghast Rubber Company.

An undisciplined, unfocused child who never graduated from high school, Tillinghast hung around with "wealthy, arrogant, flashy, reckless, heavy drinking playboys," according to his grandson, Dr. Philip Brown, Jr., of Rochester, Minn. He married Lillian Quigley in 1894, and two years later Ben Tillinghast, who had introduced his son to golf, took the young married couple to Scotland, where the younger Tillinghast discovered his life's passion. At the Old Course at St. Andrews, Tillinghast met and befriended Old Tom Morris, the game's first significant greenkeeper, club maker, golf instructor and course designer. After a half-dozen annual trips to Scotland, Tillinghast wrote: "Playing around the Old Course at St. Andrews with the patriarch made me feel as though my own game must seem glaringly new, just like walking up the church aisle in new, squeaky boots, but this feeling soon vanished. The old man and I were just boys together, for such is golf and such was Old Tom Morris."

Tillinghast biographer Philip Young said Tilly learned through Old Tom Morris that "a real man was serious and worked hard at his game and craft. He also credited Tom with inspiring a love of course design."

His obsession with golf began with, but was certainly not limited to, his skills as a player. Hannigan called him "one of the very early good (but not great) players in America." Between 1905 and 1912 he lost close matches in the U.S. Amateur to Walter Travis, H. Chandler Egan and Chick Evans; all champions. In 1910 he finished 25th in the U.S. Open.

As a photographer, Tilly used the best equipment to take superb pictures of golfers and courses in Scotland. He wrote humorous fiction about golf, described by his daughter, Elsie, as "immense, gushing sentimentalism." As a reporter and editor, he produced a syndicated column and published respected annual rankings of the top twelve American professionals, amateurs and women amateurs. He contributed to and popularized the growing lexicon of golf, including the term "birdie," which he and his Philadelphia golfing pals claim to have invented during a round in 1903. He was a tireless promoter of public golf, and owned a combination miniature golf course-driving range with lights and covered stalls. He was also one of the founders of the PGA of America.

He is remembered and revered today, however, as one of the greatest golf course architects of all time. After his second visit to St. Andrews in 1898, Tilly designed his first golf course. Ten years later he wrote: "I was invited to run out to Frankford, a suburb of Philadelphia where at that time golf had yet to be introduced. Selecting the most available ground, I laid out a rather crude course, using for holes, tin cans which had once contained French peas. With a group of curious, skeptical citizens around me I next proceeded to demonstrate the various strokes to the best of my ability until one of the spectators expressed a desire to try his hand at it."

In 1907, Tillinghast was invited to lay out a new course for wealthy industrialist Charles C. Worthington on the banks of the Delaware River at Shawnee, Pennsylvania. It was considered a groundbreaking design; Worthington invited pros from around the world to play in the inaugural Shawnee Open in 1912, an event which served notice that Tillinghast's design abilities were equal to that of the best in the British Isles. He then gained commissions to design American courses, and by the early 1920s his impressive resume included dozens of top-flight clubs. U.S. Opens and PGA Championships are still contested on his courses at Baltusrol, Winged Foot and Bethpage Black in Farmingdale, New York.

As his fame spread, so did Tilly's reputation for extravagance. "[He] could thrive on the good things—the chauffeured limousines, the staterooms on trains, the finest of three-piece suits, the best tobacco, beautiful antiques to furnish his beautiful house, and the rich and famous with whom he associated," his grandson wrote years later. The Tillinghasts lived in a handsome home in Harrington Park, in northeastern New Jersey. The stairwells and halls were covered with pictures of Lillian Russell, Jack Dempsey, Thomas Edison and other famous friends. Tillinghast had a reputation as a heavy drinker, but he stopped drinking completely in the late 1920s when he was diagnosed with heart problems.

The stock market crash of 1929 and the subsequent Depression were devastating for the golf course design business. Tilly's commissions soon dried up, and in 1936 he and Lillian were forced to leave the house in Harrington Park. At about that time, Tillinghast took a job with the PGA of America as a golf course consultant. For two years he toured the country, offering design and maintenance advice to any club that employed a PGA professional. He would faithfully report back to the PGA office after each of these visits. As the consulting work came to an end, he and Lillian moved to Beverly Hills, California, where he became an antique dealer. He suffered his first heart attack in 1940, after which he moved in with his elder daughter, Mrs. Harold Worden, in Toledo. He died of a second heart attack on May 19, 1942, and was buried at the Woodlawn Cemetery in Toledo.

Though his fame initially faded after his death, subsequent generations of golfers and golf course architecture experts have restored Tilly to his rightful place near the top of the list of great designers. In 1934, Tillinghast wrote that he had "designed and built" several hundred courses in his career. A number of those courses no longer exist, but those that do have retained their quality and charm to this day.

Tillinghast expressed his own design theories as well as any architect ever has: "If a hole does not possess a striking individuality through some gift of nature, it must be given as much as possible artificially and the artifice must be introduced in so subtle a manner as to make it seem natural."

The December 1928 issue of *10,000 Lakes Golfer* pronounced Golden Valley's new course ready for play, with seven completely new holes, and only three of the remaining holes untouched. "The Club's aim was to make every hole a good hole, with championship specifications throughout and no soft spots, with balance and no short cuts on dogleg holes," the Twin Cities-based magazine reported. "Distance has been added and the natural possibilities of the course have been utilized fully.

"Number one is seventy yards longer, with a new green. Number two is longer by one hundred yards, while on Number three the tee has been set back twenty yards and nearer the road at a new angle to the fairway. The fourth hole is a new dogleg two-shotter. Number five also is new, a one-shotter to a redan green. Number six has a new tee, while the green is in the valley below the old sixth tee, the hole being several yards longer. Number seven is another new hole, a right dogleg, over the creek with the green just short of the ninth fairway. The eighth hole, a one-shotter, will use the old green, which has been made over. The old seventh and eighth holes were eliminated.

"Numbers nine, ten and eleven are unchanged (earlier reports said a new green would be built nearer the creek on ten). The twelfth has been provided with a new green on the site of the old clubhouse. Numbers thirteen and fourteen were in play most of 1928, both being new holes; the old thirteenth green was eliminated. The fifteenth has been lengthened by one hundred and twenty yards and no longer is a drive and a pitch.

"No two holes draw more favorable comment than the sixteenth and seventeenth. On the sixteenth, the fairway has been cut through a grove, the shot to a new green on a hillside being guarded by trees on the left and right. Number seventeen is a full carry iron shot to a small green protected by flank traps and a grassy hollow behind it. Number eighteen has been lengthened into a real three-shotter as a finishing hole."

Tillinghast's design at Golden Valley would be known for deep bunkers with grass faces, and for its steeply-pitched greens. It was not a course for the timid or the frail; ladders were built into several of the bunkers to help golfers get into and out of them.

The routing proved ideal; on a course that had been re-routed a half-dozen times in its first ten years, only the par-three eighth hole – with a new green – has been altered since Tillinghast conceived of his design in 1926. A Minneapolis newspaper reporter was effusive in his praise for the new course.

#17 was typical for Tillinghast's greens and bunkers at Golden Valley
Courtesy: GVGCC

"These greens have a finesse of slope and contour that gives them a character all their own. The traps are of a decidedly bold structure and set tightly to the green. They are deep and wide and have often been referred to as "He-Man's" Hazards. The explosion shot must be in your bag. Tillinghast traps are severe but they are set, not to spoil a good shot, but to compensate a good shot as against an inferior one.

"It takes courage to build a Tillinghast course. When Golden Valley started building these greens quite a few members grew faint-hearted at such boldness and severity. But after playing them awhile the added tingle and increased thrill that goes with the shot to the green, only augmented the natural job of golfing. While severe around the greens, Tillinghast believes in little or no hazards for the weak hitter off the tees. He contends that a weak hitter handicaps himself enough as to distance. He avoids cross hazards except for the par shooter. To play a score of par at Golden Valley the golfer must have plenty of distance and be possessed of a nerve and accuracy in his shots to the green."

1930 Bird's Eye View of Golden Valley Golf Club
Courtesy: GVGCC

While the new design was being constructed, the membership was embroiled in another heated controversy over whether or not to put up a fence along the roads that bordered the course, as some believed the expense would be too great. While the sides argued back and forth, one of the Board members signed a contract to have a fence installed. The Board member had a friend who had loaned the Club $5,000 for a different purpose. Since the money hadn't been used yet, the Board member thought it should be used to build the fence. The contractor began installing the fence, which led to angry questions from members and Board members alike about who was running the Club. Nonetheless, the fence proved to be so skillfully installed, pleasing to the eye and beneficial to the Club that it was allowed to stand.

Otis George was replaced as head pro in 1927 by Bim Lovekin, who arrived from Milwaukee. He was inheriting what looked to be an ideal situation: The Club's finances were finally in good order, with a full complement of 425 playing members and a waiting list. Their classic A.W. Tillinghast golf course would be ready for its first full season of play in 1929.

A feeler was put out to the Minnesota Golf Association about hosting the 1929 State Amateur at Golden Valley, if the Town & Country Club felt its course was not in adequate shape to host the event. Golden Valley did not get that tournament, but the new Tillinghast layout did receive its first competitive test later that year when Gertrude Boothby of Rochester Country Club won the Women's State Amateur at Golden Valley, defeating Mrs. Dow George of the Country Club 4 & 3.

Golden Valley put in another losing bid to host the 1930 Men's Amateur – it went to Rochester Country Club (the other new Tillinghast course in Minnesota) – but soon the Club would have far bigger issues to deal with.

A Bim Lovekin Cleek
Courtesy: Joe Gladke

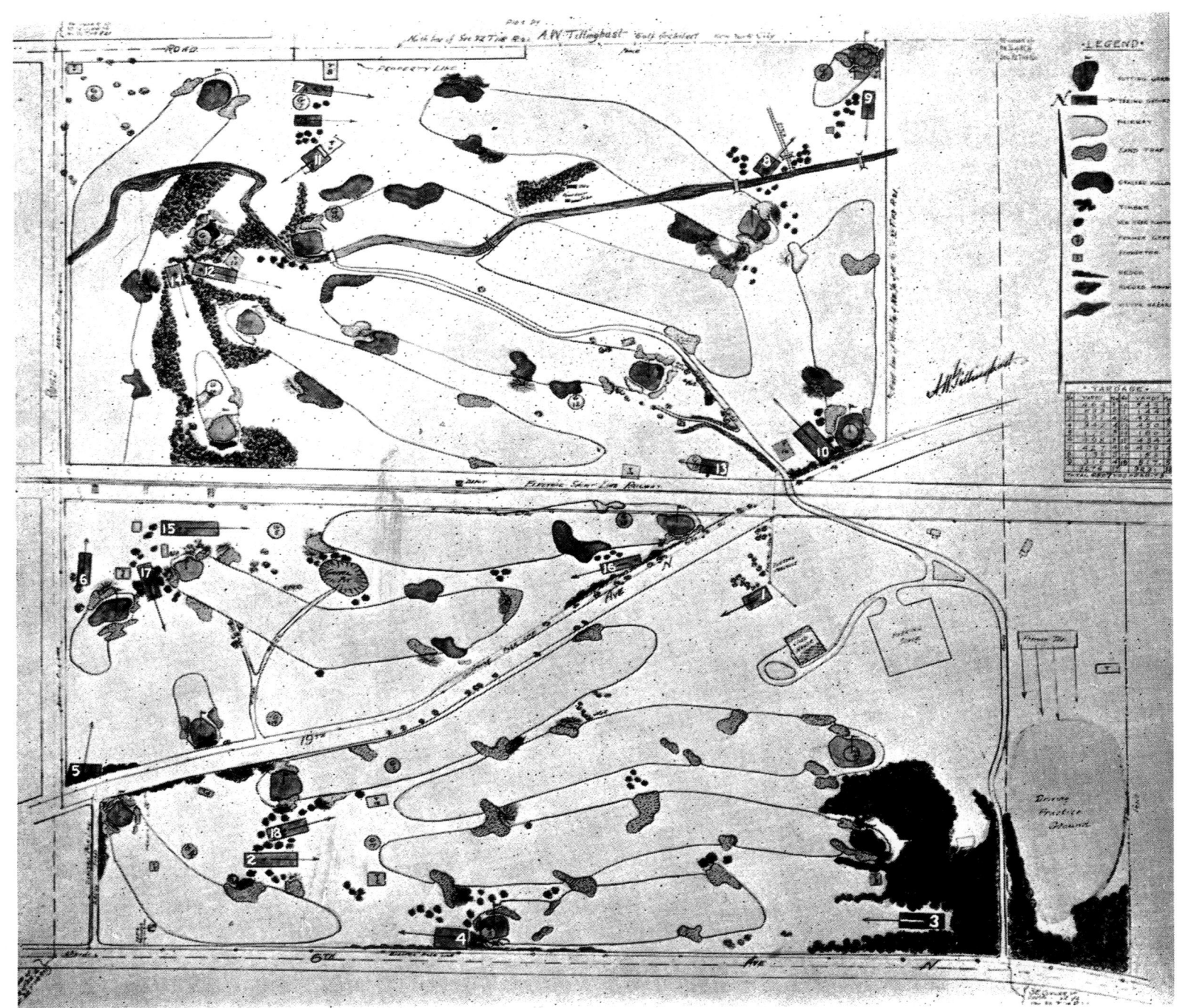

Tillinghast Plan of Golden Valley Golf Club
Courtesy: GVGCC

PART THREE ⁓
HARD TIMES

On October 29, 1929, the crash of the U. S. Stock Market meant an abrupt end to the economic euphoria that had swept the country along since the end of World War I. Suddenly, banks failed, jobs disappeared and homes went into foreclosure. No segment of society was untouched; golf was no exception.

Yet in 1930, the scope of the crisis was not fully apparent. Many held onto their private club memberships, hoping the nation's economy would soon rebound. The State Open was played at Golden Valley, where an unattached pro from Minneapolis named George Baening shot a ten-over par 302 to win the four-round stroke-play event. Golden Valley head pro Bim Lovekin fired the lowest score of the second round, a 72, but didn't finish in the top ten. Town and Country's Jock Hendry, who also finished out of the top ten, shot a 69 in the third round for the tournament low.

The big golf news that summer was the emergence of young Pat Sawyer of Golden Valley as the state's new star. Just seventeen years old, Sawyer won the first of his four State Amateur championships at Rochester Golf and Country Club.

Pat Sawyer

Pat Sawyer
Courtesy: GVGCC

Pat Sawyer was born on St. Patrick's Day 1913, and though he was christened Charles Martius Sawyer, he was always known as Pat. Golf was a family passion for the Sawyers. Father Charles W. Sawyer was a founding member of Golden Valley, and Pat's brothers Walt and Dick were also fine players – Dick won the 1936 State Amateur.

"Dad always played Saturdays and Sundays, and he'd take me with him to the Club to get me out of mother's hair," Sawyer told author George E. Brown III in 100 Years of Minnesota Golf. "He would turn me over to the general manager and his wife [Cliff and Emma Miller] and I'd sit in the kitchen and watch Emma make cookies for Sunday dinner."

Sawyer learned how to properly grip a club from Jimmy Dyer and Jock Slater, Otis George's assistants. He joined the MGA at age nine and played in his first tournament, the inaugural State Junior Championship, at age eleven. He shot 111, but rather than be discouraged, he exhibited a lifelong characteristic of learning from experience and using it for motivation. He would carry a handful of clubs and ride his bike from his home in South Minneapolis to the Luce Electric Line on North Seventh Street then ride the train to the golf course, where he would play until the last train headed back to town. While at West High School in Minneapolis, he organized a golf league at Glenwood Golf Club in which the boys would play all day for fifty cents.

As teenaged Pat burned his way across Minnesota's golf courses, the press dubbed him The Boy Wonder. He won the state Junior Championship in both 1929 and 1930, the Resorters Tournament in Alexandria in 1930, the first two Pine to Palms in Detroit Lakes in 1930 and 1931, and won the state high school championship in 1931. In 1929 he took on the state's best, reaching the quarter-finals of the 1929 State Amateur. Although he was soundly defeated 11 & 9 in that match by another great young Minnesota star, Les Bolstad, the always resilient Sawyer came back even more determined the following year at the Rochester Golf and Country Club and won the championship by defeating Art Tveraa of The Country Club 6 & 4 in the finals. Tveraa had defeated Don Burris of Golden Valley 2 & 1 to reach the championship match, while the seventeen-year-old Sawyer thumped Jake Wetherby 7 & 6. Sawyer remains the youngest player ever to win the Minnesota State Amateur Championship.

Sawyer did not fizzle after his spectacular start. He won the State Amateur again in 1932, defeating Lee Herron of Interlachen 2 & 1 in the finals at Midland Hills.

"Few matched Pat's steadiness," wrote James Kelley in Minnesota Golf: Ninety Years of Tournament History. "He had all the shots, could finesse the ball and was an exquisite putter. The guy rarely beat himself, probably because no one was more relaxed on a golf course. It was all fun. His infectious smile was the clue."

Sawyer qualified for the U.S. Amateur every year from 1932 to 1935, tied for fifty-second at the 1933 U.S. Open, and won his first Minnesota State Open in 1935, firing a two-under par 290 at the Minikahda Club. He turned pro the following year, and won the State Open again, this time at Golden Valley where he was now the head pro. He challenged the best touring pros at the 1937 St. Paul Open at Keller Golf Course, finishing third behind winner Sam Snead. He also tied for sixteenth at the 1937 U.S. Open at Oakland Hills, after having been just two shots off the lead at the halfway point.

"We're going along and I shoot 142 for the first two rounds," Sawyer was quoted in *100 Years of Minnesota Golf*. "The talk at the tournament was about this young upstart coming down from Minnesota. Then the pairings came out for the last day and I played with Sam Snead the last two rounds. What a thrill it was for me."

He played in his only PGA Championship in 1939. He also returned to the U.S. Open that year, tying for forty-seventh. He missed the cut at the 1940 U.S. Open, and qualified for the Open a final time in 1949, yet withdrew.

Sawyer left Golden Valley in 1939 for the head pro job at Birmingham Country Club outside Detroit, and spent the war years playing the winter professional tour in the South. He traveled with and played against pros Snead, Craig Wood and Henry Picard, and became friends with the retired Bobby Jones, who invited him to stay at his home in Atlanta and play together at Jones's home course, East Lake Country Club. "He was a wonderful guy, and I was just in awe of him," Sawyer recalled.

Sawyer regained his amateur status in 1946, and resumed his dominance over the local competition. That year, playing as a member of Interlachen, he finished second in the State Open and won his third State Amateur. He won his fourth and final State Amateur in 1948 at Interlachen, beating Kenny Young of Golden Valley 5 & 4 in the finals. From 1947 to 1951, he won a record five straight Resorters Tournaments, and won again in 1954. He also qualified for the U.S. Amateur four more times, in 1949, 1950, 1952 & 1954.

Sawyer's last hurrah came in 1956, fittingly enough at Golden Valley: He returned to his boyhood home to win his third State Open title at the age of forty-three. Though Sawyer was no longer a member, the familiar surroundings must have stirred memories of so many youthful triumphs. Three shots off the lead going into the third and final round, Sawyer shot a sizzling five-under 68 to nip Ade Simonsen by a stroke.

Sawyer once again turned pro, working out of Minnesota Valley and Lost Spur in the late 1950s and early 1960s, during which time he racked up five more top-ten finishes in State Opens, but his winning days had come to an end. He won a total of seven Minnesota majors — four State Amateurs and three State Opens — in a quarter-century span from 1930 to 1956.

In his later years, Sawyer was an Edina resident and played golf into his nineties at the Braemar Golf Course. He died on April 30, 2003.

He was inducted into the Minnesota PGA-MGA Hall of Fame in 1992.

The 1931 Trans-Mississippi

The only time the prestigious Trans-Mississippi Amateur Championship has come to Golden Valley was in 1931, two years after A. W. Tillinghast's new design had opened. Who better to tame this tough course than the red-hot Pat Sawyer, who knew it inside and out and played it better than anyone? Yet when the tournament began, Pat's brother Dick, playing out of The Country Club of Edina, led the first round of qualifying by shooting even-par 73 on the course where he learned the game. He bogeyed three holes but then chipped in for an eagle on the thirteenth hole. Minnesota's other main hope, Les Bolstad, was five shots back after shooting a 78.

Medalist honors went to Johnny Goodman of Omaha, who won the title in 1927 and became a national star when he knocked Bobby Jones out of the 1929 U.S. Amateur at Pebble Beach. Goodman shot a three-under-par 70 on the second day of qualifying to tie the amateur course record established by Billy Sixty of Milwaukee.

Once match play began, Goodman and Bolstad seemed to be on a collision course. Goodman eliminated Interlachen's Allan LaBatt 2 up, and defeated Denmar Miller of Des Moines, Iowa 4 & 2. During the quarter-finals, "A stiff wind cut across most fairways and played havoc with almost every wood shot," according to the Associated Press. Yet Goodman took five of the first seven holes and halved the others on the more difficult front nine in the morning round. He shot two under par on the front nine in the afternoon to eliminate Earl Larson of Minneapolis, 7 & 6. Goodman then defeated Fred Dold of Wichita, Kansas in the semis to set up a final-round match with Bolstad, who had knocked off Dr. Paul Barton, the Iowa Amateur champion.

Bolstad, who would become Golden Valley's head pro from 1945 to 1946 after stops at Westwood Hills and Minneapolis Golf Club, had been a teen prodigy much like Pat Sawyer. He won the first Minnesota Junior Championship in 1924 and reached the finals of the 1925 State Amateur, where he was defeated by Jimmy Johnston. He was captain of the University of Minnesota golf team for three years, winning two Big Ten individual championships; he won the Minnesota Public Golf Association championship in both 1925 and 1926, and in 1926 he won the U.S. Public Links championship in Buffalo, New York. He won the Minnesota State Amateur in 1931 and would eventually win four State Opens and two Minnesota PGAs as well.

Bolstad stumbled out of the gate against Goodman, going three down after the morning eighteen, and never led in the match. Goodman's game slipped on the front nine of the afternoon round. According to the AP reporter, Bolstad outplayed him tee to green on virtually every hole. "However, the St. Paul man could not make his putter perform and went into the final nine still three down." Bolstad had to pick up on both the eleventh and twelfth holes; he managed to stave off the inevitable by birdieing the par-5 thirteenth, but on the treacherous par-3 fourteenth, Goodman holed a curling, sidehill twenty-footer for birdie that gave him the 5 & 4 victory.

Two years later, Goodman won the 1933 U.S. Open, the last time an amateur has won the Open. Bolstad, still an amateur, finished tied for 19th at that Open.

Final Scene of the 1931 Trans - Mississippi Amateur Championship
Courtesy: GVGCC

After Pat Sawyer's stunning victory in the 1930 State Amateur, the Golden Valley board voted him a lifetime membership. Four years later, however, the Club's declining fortunes forced the board to withdraw his and all other honorary memberships.

Throughout the 1930s, the membership level at the Club continued to drop. Even though the cost of belonging to Golden Valley was less than any other Minneapolis club, the total membership continued to slip. There had been 244 regular members at the time of the Club's annual meeting in December 1933; by January 1934, there had been fifty-six resignations, leaving the membership level at 188. Necessary maintenance was done to keep the Club up and running (including a new clubhouse roof), but the outlook was dire.

The Club's president in 1934 was Austen Cargill, son of the founder of the Cargill Corporation. With extreme alarm, Cargill viewed the impending demise of his golf club. At an invitation-only dinner hosted by the Board of Governors in January 1934, Cargill recapped the recent annual meeting, at which the Club decided it would be better off with a restricted membership than trying to maintain a large number of members among whom to spread out the costs of operation.

At that meeting, Cargill discussed whether the club should concentrate on being an exclusive golf club catering primarily to men, or a more-broad-based organization appealing to a wider variety of members – issues that would be debated at Golden Valley for decades to come.

"I knew something was wrong and that it couldn't be laid to the Depression when I considered the way other golf clubs had been able to replace the members they lost from financial reverses, while Golden Valley, with the best golf course and lowest dues of all, couldn't hold its membership within sixty percent of its former level," Cargill said.

His conclusion was that the membership mix at Golden Valley simply wasn't working: "It is possible for every single member of Golden Valley to be a mighty fine, worthwhile fellow individually, but when you mix us all up together as we are when we consider the Club as a whole, the result is not satisfactory, and, in my opinion, the trouble with Golden Valley Golf Club is the fact it hasn't any character – good, bad or indifferent."

To rectify that flaw, Cargill told the dinner attendees that the Club would no longer attempt to maintain any set membership level, and would no longer attempt to recruit new members. In fact, the Board was "removing all resistance against resignations and each individual is, so far as the Board is concerned, perfectly free to get out, or stay in, just as he pleases," Cargill said. "No one knows what is going to be the final result, but I think one thing is certain, and that is that when you meld together the remaining members, you will have a club with a well-defined character."

Cargill wanted a club that appealed primarily to men who could afford to pay more to have fewer members. Yet he was not opposed to adding more like-minded members.

"While our new policy prevents the Club from recruiting new members, there is no reason why the members can't do it in their individual capacities," he said. "Surely, we all have golfing friends who may or may not belong to other clubs that would be interested in Golden Valley if they knew what it had to offer. When I think of our fine golf course, our locker room converted into attractive, comfortable quarters for the male members, the freedom from congestion both on and off the golf course, which our limited membership guarantees, and the high grade character the Club is going to have in the future, it not only makes a very attractive picture to me, but it revives the enthusiasm and high hopes I had for Golden Valley when I first joined it."

Austen Cargill

Austen Cargill
Courtesy: GVGCC

Austen Cargill was the youngest son of William Wallace Cargill, who in 1865 founded the family grain business, now a multi-national agricultural company that is the largest privately held corporation in the United States.

The company headquartered in LaCrosse, Wisconsin, when John H. MacMillan, Sr., began working for William Cargill and his brother Sam. MacMillan married William Cargill's eldest daughter, Edna, moved to Minneapolis and, after William Cargill died in 1909, ran the company until his death in 1936.

Austen Cargill began working for the family business in 1913, first in Green Bay and then in Milwaukee. In 1917 he went overseas to serve in the U.S. Army during World War I, as did John MacMillan's son, John Jr. According to the book "Cargill Going Global," by Wayne G. Broehl, Jr., "Austen Cargill ... gravitated toward the periphery of the organization, focusing his attentions particularly on branch offices. He became a popular person among company personnel and proved to be the most outgoing and organizationally sensitive person among the family members who were in management."

Austen oversaw the family's lumber business in British Columbia until he returned to the Twin Cities full time in 1926 to oversee the company's grain elevators. He helped the company maneuver through credit crunches and foreclosures during the Depression, and attempted to do the same as president of the Golden Valley Golf Club. He made numerous loans to the Club to keep it solvent; it is not an exaggeration to say that Cargill's generosity saved the Golden Valley Golf Club from extinction. When the Club undertook new ownership in 1941, Austen Cargill retained the highest number of shares, but he ceased to be a vocal leader at the Club. He retained his membership when the Club was purchased by members of the Zuhrah Shrine in 1950. When he died in 1957, a $100,000 loan he made to the Club back in the 1930s was written off, with no interest ever paid.

With annual dues at $120 per year, Cargill estimated that 230 members would be enough to sustain an excellent level of service and rebuild the locker room. The Club could get by with 180 members, Cargill, said, but at any number below that, "the Club is going to need some help."

That help would come from Cargill himself. Along with Guy Masters, vice-president of Northwestern National Bank, Cargill made a series of loans to the Club, and 25 members bought extra shares of stock to keep Golden Valley Golf Club from becoming a nightclub.

Cargill's less-is-more approach, and his loans, kept the doors open for a few more years, but the struggling economy kept pushing the Club closer and closer to the brink. Pat Sawyer couldn't afford to keep playing competitive golf for nothing, so he turned pro in 1936. His fellow Club members wasted no time naming him their head pro, replacing Lovekin.

In May of 1936, Tillinghast traveled to the Twin Cities. His first stop was an interview on WCCO radio to discuss his new job as a consultant for the PGA of America, in which he visited affiliated golf clubs across America and offered suggestions on how to improve their courses. The next day he made his return to the Golden Valley Golf Club, where the local section of the PGA was holding its first tournament of the year.

Tillinghast would have normally toured the course with Sawyer, discussing details of the layout and suggesting modifications as needed. But this visit was merely to get acquainted with the other PGA pros of the area.

"While I planned this course ten years ago I refrained from extending our PGA service there, for Pat Sawyer has not yet qualified as a PGA member, although he will do so when he is eligible," Tillinghast reported to the PGA. "He only entered the profession last January. However, at a meeting in the clubhouse [local PGA] president Willie Kidd introduced me to the members and I gave them a talk concerning our service and its motive. Kidd is to collect all requests for attention when I return here as I swing back later."

Tillinghast never did return to the Golden Valley course, however. Had he visited in 1937, he would surely have been dismayed to learn that president George C. Wright and the Board of Directors had authorized the partial filling of "the exceptionally deep" bunkers on many holes. "Others will be treated likewise to fit the wishes of the average golfer," Wright informed the membership. The softening of Tillinghast's masterpiece had begun.

Wright expressed optimism that the Club was on solid footing in his 1937 annual report. "When you consider that your Club has reduced its capital indebtedness $31,000 during the dark years of the Depression, continuing to carry on the high standard of your Club life and establishing a true spirit of good fellowship, we can well stop to peruse with considerable satisfaction," Wright said.

Wright, too, touched on issues that would be revisited again and again in the club's future:

By 1937, club officials had begun filling Tillinghast's bunkers such as these on the second and third holes
Courtesy: GVGCC

"Golden Valley has more to offer in golf than any club in this section of the country. Ladies' social functions are limited, but pleasant; we do not aim to excel in this branch of activity but we do have golf for men, ladies, juniors and children, the like of no other facilities available. Women and junior play is regulated to hours similar to other leading golf clubs. During 1936 you have enjoyed the privilege of playing more golf in a shorter space of time than ever offered before – no Saturday, Sunday or holiday starting time – no necessity for prearranged games – no cluttering of the course, allowing time on Saturday for an extra hour of bridge and Sunday an equivalent amount of time to spend with the family."

Wright also addressed the plans to widen and straighten Olson Memorial Highway, passing the Club immediately to the south, "making it possible to reach the Club from anywhere in the loop district within ten minutes."

He informed the Club that Pat Sawyer ("now of international fame") would return for his second season as head pro in 1937, with Ray Keller ("exceptionally popular last year") as his assistant pro and Mike Sanko returning as greenkeeper.

"Lighthorse" Harry Cooper

Born Harry E. Cooper in Leatherhead, England, in 1904, Cooper was described in his New York Times obituary as "the hard-luck Hall of Fame golfer" who won 31 PGA Tour events, but never a major.

He was nicknamed "Lighthorse" at the 1926 Los Angeles Open by newspaperman Damon Runyon, who told Cooper he needed a horse to keep up with the fast-walking, fast-playing Englishman. Cooper took just two and a half hours to defeat George Von Elm in an eighteen-hole playoff to win that L.A. Open, the first U.S. professional event with a $10,000 purse.

Harry Cooper
Courtesy: Associated Press

Cooper's father had served as an apprentice to Old Tom Morris at The Old Course at St. Andrews, Scotland. His mother, Alice, was also a golf professional. When Harry was ten, his father moved the family to Dallas, Texas, where he took a job as a club professional. Harry Cooper followed his parents into the golf profession in 1923. He won the Galveston Open that year at the age of nineteen for his first victory, and became a steady winner on the fledgling U.S. pro tour. Minnesota seemed to be a particular favorite stop for Cooper; he won the inaugural St. Paul Open in 1930, and became the event's only three-time winner with triumphs in 1934 and 1936. Indeed, the tournament was jokingly referred to as the "Cooper Annuity" because of his success there.

Cooper's competitive career peaked in 1937, when he won eight tournaments, the Vardon Trophy for lowest scoring average, and was first on the money list with more than $14,000. He had seven top-ten finishes in the U.S. Open, but the title always eluded him — perhaps most bitterly in 1927 and 1936 when he sat in the clubhouse with final-round leads, only to eventually lose to later finishers. He also lost the 1936 Masters by one shot after holding the third-round lead.

"'I still dwell on the big ones that got away,' Cooper later said.

"Coopy was a great shotmaker, one of the three best fairway-wood players ever with Bobby Jones and Byron Nelson," said contemporary pro Paul Runyan. "But he thought that everybody else got all the breaks and he never got any."

After previous club pro jobs in Illinois, Cooper ran the Golden Valley Golf Club pro shop from 1942 to 1944. His contacts on the PGA tour were instrumental in establishing the two-year run of The Golden Valley Invitational, a professional four-ball tournament. He also won the Minnesota State Open at The Country Club in Edina in 1942.

After leaving Golden Valley, he was head professional at the Oahu Country Club in Hawaii, and later was a teaching pro at Westchester Country Club in Rye, New York, until his death in 2000 at the age of 96.

The first year of the new ownership at Golden Valley Golf Club was relatively successful. At the annual meeting, treasurer Kunz reported a profit of $8,565 through December 20, 1941. There were 9,417 rounds of golf played in 1941. More bunkers were altered or eliminated during the season, and a new tee was built on the seventh hole. Guy Masters reported on prospects for golf in 1942, drawing a comparison between problems during the First World War and the present war, which had been declared little more than a month earlier. He stressed the necessity of keeping up morale, and discussed the importance of the conservation of gas and tires, considering the accessibility of Golden Valley's golf course to Minneapolis. He said the Club had 229 golf members, and urged everyone to try to find new members for the coming season.

President Cameron's address was as upbeat as one could expect after the financial difficulties of 1940 and the outbreak of a second World War: "I cannot imagine where anyone can get a greater kick out of life than by getting together with a bunch of jolly good fellows and planning together and working together to develop the ideas that are designed to afford so much pleasure and enjoyment to both the members, their families, and golfing cronies..."

Cameron took pride in the progress made during the past year. He crowed that Harry Cooper's signing at Golden Valley was featured on the first page – "in large type" – of Golfdom magazine.

"We know now that we have a valuable or worthwhile investment," Cameron said. "But little did we dream that we were going to attract nation-wide attention and have leading members of the golfing fraternity knocking at our door. Where do we go from here? With what we have to offer for a golf course, together with the national prominence that we have attained through having contracted one of the outstanding golf pros, we must now be far-sighted enough to make the most of our possibilities."

Then he permitted himself to start dreaming Cargill-like dreams of creating the perfect golf club:

"I am convinced that we could redecorate and equip our club rooms so as to make ours one of the most attractive cocktail lounges and dining rooms of any club in the Twin Cities at little or no cost to ourselves, through selling limited social privileges ... We are closest to the city. We have one of the sportiest courses. Grand locker room facilities. Modern equipment for maintaining the course. Careful management. Capable greens keeper. Good watering system. Shrubbery, trees and flower gardens. Increasing list of playing members ...

It would not be difficult to imagine that our Club would do other than continue to expand and prosper. Since the advent of our present Board administration, the grounds including the fairways, greens, sidewalks, and roads have been put in shape; the trees, shrubs and flower beds have been cultivated and kept trimmed; the buildings have been repaired and painted; and some improvements have been made inside the clubhouse; and new machinery bought and paid for. The grill room can be made much more attractive. This can be done if the bunch of us will get busy and fill up the membership."

Unfortunately, 1942 was not as successful as the previous year. The plan to sell home sites stalled due to wartime restrictions. The membership dropped to 174 by December, and rounds were down to 8,140. In March, the Club hired a new couple to run the kitchen and dining room, but they quit after three weeks. The Club then gave the job back to Emma Miller, who had run the clubhouse with her husband Cliff as far back as 1919.

Changes to the golf course were being considered to help combat dwindling numbers. "Some objection has been raised to length of holes and we were considering having two sets of tee markers and having a red course and a white course," the committee reported. "This will make one course several shots easier and will meet the demands of both types of players. This has been adopted in several clubs in the east and has been fairly successful."

Other postponed changes were geared toward further softening Tillinghast's design, due to increased complaints from members that the golf course was too difficult. A sand bunker 350 yards from the tee on the first hole was to be turned into a grassy hollow; the bunker floors around the second green were to be raised; two "eyebrow traps" on the third hole were to

The early forties brought further softening of Tilinghast's features. Bunkers on hole #12 and elsewhere were to become grassy hollows.
Courtesy: GVGCC

be filled in; sand bunkers on holes nine, ten, twelve and thirteen were to be converted to grassy hollows; and out-of-bounds left of the ninth fairway was deemed unnecessary.

At the annual meeting, Arthur Statt reported that income was down in 1942 compared to the previous year, but so were expenses. The food service lost $2,557.96, but the greens committee saved $3,790, primarily because they decided to put off the planned changes to the course. "We felt some uncertainty as to income, due to our nation being at war and decided that conservatism should be the order of the day." Some of the golf course work was done in 1943.

Further belt-tightening and revenue-generating ideas were necessary as the war dragged into its second year. Beginning April 15, Emma Miller operated the cafeteria on a limited menu, and the main dining room was closed except for special occasions. Statt and Harry Cooper installed cards in area hotel rooms inviting guests to play at the Club for the regular guest fee. Per his request, Cooper's hours were adjusted, reducing his salary from $2,500 to $2,000 for the season.

Bing Crosby, Midland Hills Pro Wally Mund, GVGCC Pro Harry Cooper and Bob Hope
Courtesy: GVGCC

The softening of the golf course came at a curious point in the Club's history. By the summer of 1943, Golden Valley Golf Club was in negotiations with the PGA of America to host a professional tournament. The St. Paul Open was on hiatus due to the war, giving Golden Valley an opportunity to showcase its golf course and make some much-needed revenue from gate receipts.

Harry Cooper was essential to the success of the proposal. If he could persuade his friends from the pro tour to come to Minnesota, the Club members had no doubt that galleries would flock to Golden Valley to watch them play. The Twin Cities had always been a hotbed of golf enthusiasm, dating back to the 1916 U.S. Open and 1927 U.S. Amateur at Minikahda and the 1930 U.S. Open at Interlachen. The St. Paul Open had drawn consistently good crowds beginning in 1930, despite the Depression. A limited-field pro event at Golden Valley seemed like a can't-miss idea.

On August 10, the Board gave its unanimous approval to what would be called The Golden Valley Invitational, consisting of "sixteen players selected from the best pros of the United States" competing in a two-man best-ball format. The tournament would be held on September 3-6. Each pro was to be paid $250 up front, and would play for $5,000 face value War Bonds as prizes. The event was sponsored by the War Chest of Minneapolis and Hennepin County, which would receive all net receipts, determined by the gross income from ticket sales minus the cost of staging the tournament. Expectations were rosy for the financial success of the event. The Board estimated $20,000 in ticket sales, with expenses of $9,000 for prize money and appearance fees, $2,000 in admission tax, $500 in travel expenses, $1,000 in printing costs for tickets and advertising, $500 for ticket sales and gate men, and $1,000 to reinforce the course's bridges. Estimated net profit: $6,000.

To protect the Club, Golden Valley Associates was guaranteed "a sinking fund of $10,000 by certain members of the Golden Valley Golf Club."

Golden Valley hoped to take its profit from the sale of two-dollar clubhouse passes, parking fees of twenty-five cents each, and the net profit from food and beverage sales in the clubhouse and on the grounds. Craig Wood and Jimmy Demaret won the event, but dreadful weather turned the event into a financial disaster.

In his annual report at the end of 1943, President Cameron chose to emphasize the positive, despite wartime difficulties. "A trying war year passed with its diversion of food, labor, gasoline, and supplies," he said. "We have patiently borne with each other our not-too-serious inconveniences. Our first consideration is the successful prosecution of the war we are engaged in, and which, when brought to a conclusion, will permit us to return to our full peacetime facilities. It is our sincere wish for you and yours a healthy, prosperous, and happy 1944."

"We had another eventful year and one that will go down as outstanding in the history of Golden Valley Golf Club. This not only applies to Golden Valley Golf Club, which gained city and nation-wide recognition for its leadership in helping to support a sporting activity known as the Golden Valley Invitational Tournament, but also considering the fact the Club has finished the year financially in the black...much credit... can be given to Manager Arthur Statt" Cameron concluded.

The Club showed an operating profit despite a membership that had dipped from 174 in December 1943 to just 140 in January 1944. Secretary Guy Masters apologized for the cutbacks in service, but said they were necessary.

"The operation of a golf club is uncertain under normal conditions, and doubly so under war conditions, when materials and supplies are rationed and labor difficult to get and members are jumpy," Masters said. "At all times it keeps the management on its toes making quick decisions in emergencies. It is not to be wondered that mistakes are made, but it is almost a miracle that more are not made. In their effort to steer our ship as best they could, your Board had eleven called meetings, averaging four hours and numerous impromptu meetings of which no record was kept.

"We endeavored to operate the Club on as conservative a basis as possible, and at times probably went too far, but please remember we did not always see enough income in sight to do otherwise without getting

THE GOLDEN VALLEY INVITATIONAL 1943-1944

It was such a good idea. Invite sixteen of the best pro golfers in America to team up for a four-day best-ball tournament at an outstanding private course in the middle of the golf-mad Twin Cities. The names still resonate: Byron Nelson. Ben Hogan. Jimmy Demaret. Craig Wood. Lloyd Mangrum. "Lighthorse" Harry Cooper. The winners would be determined by the cumulative number of holes won throughout all the matches. WTCN radio would broadcast the tournament. The local papers would give it blanket coverage. How could such an event be anything but a huge success?

Practice rounds for the first Golden Valley Invitational, in 1943, produced birdies galore, despite the sizzling afternoon temperatures. Harry Cooper and his partner Chick Harbert (who would win the 1954 PGA Championship at Keller) set the tone with a 65; Harbert knocked his second shot over the green on the par-five second hole, nearly drove into the creek more than 300 yards off the tee on the par-four seventh hole and eagled the par-five thirteenth hole with a drive and a three-iron. The following day, Toney Penna and his partner Willie Goggin warmed up with a 9-under 64.

Unfortunately, the sun and heat that had greeted the first players to visit the course on Tuesday turned to clouds and cold by Friday, and the weather only got worse as the weekend progressed.

"SCORING ORGY LIKELY AS G-V LINKS TOURNEY OPENS TODAY" read the headline in the Friday, September 3 Minneapolis Morning Tribune sports page. The prediction was accurate: Byron Nelson and his partner Harold "Jug" McSpaden fired a 62 in their opening match to defeat Wood and Demaret and take a big lead in the tournament. Nelson had been dead tired when he drove into town from Toledo on Friday morning, and was recovering from a stiff neck that made it difficult for him to move his head. Yet despite not playing the course previously, and despite incurring a penalty shot for

Byron Nelson and Henry Orme
Courtesy: GVGCC

hitting into a ditch on the 6th hole, Nelson shot 62 on his own ball – counting two conceded putts of three feet and five feet. He called it the greatest round of golf he'd ever played on a championship course.

"I was there on opening day and followed the match," longtime Golden Valley member Clayton Kaufman recalled years later. "Nelson was a machine that day."

Nelson's most memorable shot came on the difficult seventh hole, after driving behind trees on the right side of the hole. "He lined up at nearly a ninety-degree angle to the green and sharply faded a high six-iron shot to about two or three feet from the hole for a tap-in birdie," Kaufman wrote. "On the thirteenth hole, another slightly wayward drive caught the trap that's still on the right side of the fairway. From the sand,

Nelson rifled his second shot to no more than five feet from the cup – setting up an easy eagle."

Despite a rainstorm that hit the course at noon and held the gallery to just over one thousand, no team shot higher than 68. Nelson and McSpaden led after the first day with a score of +4 (determined by the number of holes they were up at the end of their match), while Wood and Demaret brought up the rear at -4. Midland Hills head pro Wally Mund, president of the local PGA, followed the matches in a microphone-equipped car and kept spectators abreast of the scoring.

Saturday was wet from start to finish – "a persistent rain that held the attendance under two thousand," according to the Tribune. Nelson and McSpaden held their three-hole lead by taking a four-hole win over White and Laffoon in the morning before dropping a match 1-up to Bill Kaiser and Johnny Revolta, who holed out three times from off the green. Cooper and Harbert were alone in second after splitting two matches. A photo on the first page of the Tribune sports section showed a soaked, shirtless Harbert, his hair plastered to his forehead yet grinning as he strode down the fairway.

Cooper had the low individual round of 64, but also was the victim of the day's most embarrassing incident. While hitting a tee shot, Harbert's club hit the saturated turf well behind his ball and slipped out of his hands; the ball moved only a foot, and the deep, wet divot smacked Cooper in the face.

The *Monday Minneapolis Tribune* dubbed it "the tournament of the Great Rains," after another day of showers. Nelson and McSpaden had upped their lead to five holes with two matches left to play on Labor Day, and the Tribune's Bernard Swanson called catching those two "a herculean job that seems comparatively insurmountable as controlling the weather." The Sam Byrd-Lloyd Mangrum duo then cruised to the round of the day with a 64 – despite a spectacular two-hole stretch by Harbert, who eagled the par-five thirteenth and then holed his tee shot on the fly on fourteen for the first ace of his career. The previous day, he'd been asked if he'd ever posted a hole-in-one, and Harbert said, "Nope, and boy, I would like to know how it feels." Apparently no sentimentalist, Harbert sold that ball to Midland Hills member Herman Laing for ten dollars.

"No golf tournament ever had experienced such all-wet difficulties as the current Golden Valley Invitational," the Tribune reported that Monday. "This is unseasonable. Fair Week usually brings the hottest weather of the year and certainly nothing like this ... But as reward for the tremendous job Golden Valley has done in the face of the most discouraging conditions possible, there already is around $8,000 in the exchequer. That means the tournament must attract better than $4,000 in the final two rounds Monday in the hope of breaking even and giving the War Chest any kind of a financial break."

Wally Mund did his best to add to the Club's take. He sat at the first tee and hawked autographed programs to the gallery. He raised a total of sixty-two dollars on Sunday, thanks largely to the sale of ten programs signed by Byron Nelson.

The weather was dreary again on Labor Day (described as "lachrymose skies and crippling cold" by the Tribune), but the golf was anything but dreary. Craig Wood and Jimmy Demaret dominated in two matches to pass Nelson and McSpaden and win the 1943 Golden Valley Invitational by three holes, with a score of +12 (holes). The winning team needed help from Goggin and Penna, who teamed for a remarkable six-under-par 30 on the back nine against Nelson and McSpaden. Goggin made twenty-footers on twelve and seventeen, while Penna made putts of twelve, ten, and fifteen feet, then sealed Nelson and

McSpaden's doom with a four-footer for birdie on eighteen.

Wood and Demaret took the first-place prize of $1,200 in War Bonds. Penna greeted Wood and Demaret with a grin when they finished, telling them: "Here I am, boys. You better kiss me for dropping that last putt." Nelson and McSpaden had a tournament-low scoring average but still came in second, earning $1,000.

Despite the weather – which he said was not the worst he'd played in – Mangrum told the reporters that the pros would rather play in the Twin Cities than anywhere else: "They're the two best golfing towns in the country, and we are treated here the best, too."

1943 GOLDEN VALLEY INVITATIONAL FINAL STANDINGS
(BY NUMBER OF WINNING HOLES):

WOOD-DEMARET	+12
NELSON-MCSPADEN	+9
BYRD-MANGRUM	+7
TURNESA-TURNESA	Even
COOPER-HARBERT	-4
REVOLTA-KAISER	-6
WHITE-LAFFOON	-7
PENNA-GOGGIN	-11

But would they come back? And would Golden Valley Golf Club be willing to take a chance on hosting the tournament again? All of the guarantors lost their money due to poor weather and low attendance.

After all the numbers were in, on October 15, 1943, President Cameron reported to the Board that "The tournament was very successful in every direction except financially." The Club was not willing to give up on the Invitational, however. A committee was appointed to try to find enough members willing to act as guarantors for the 1944 tournament, any proceeds from which would be used to pay off the 1943 guarantors, who had lost approximately $9,000. Remarkably, the Club was able to find twenty-four members to act as 1944 guarantors, half putting up $250 and the other half putting up $500.

The PGA agreed to give the Club the dates of July sixth through ninth, almost ensuring better weather. The total purse would be $6,000, with the top prize set at $1,600 in War Bonds, followed by $1,200 for second and $1,000 for third.

In March, invitations were sent to previous participants Cooper, Nelson, Wood, Penna, Revolta, McSpaden, Harbert, Byrd, Goggin, Kaiser and Mike Turnesa, and to Jimmy Hines, Ellsworth Vines, Johnny Bulla, Joe Kirkwood, Ed Dudley, Olin Dutra and Bob Hamilton.

The war had an even greater effect on the 1944 edition of the Invitational. Sam Snead was serving in the Navy in San Diego, where he'd suffered a back injury. Ben Hogan was in the Army Air Corps in Texas. Lloyd Mangrum was not invited to return because he was on active duty with the U.S. Army. He had been offered the head pro job at the Fort Meade golf course in Maryland, but chose to continue to train for overseas combat. By the time the 1944 Golden Valley Invitational was held, Mangrum had already participated in the D-Day landings in France. He would later be wounded at the Battle of the Bulge and win two Purple Hearts for his service. After resuming his golf career, he won the 1946 U.S. Open.

Penna, Revolta and McSpaden quickly accepted their invitations; Wood declined. The field was announced as Nelson and McSpaden, Revolta and Byrd, Hines and Goggin, Cooper and Vines, Kaiser and Hamilton, Harbert and Turnesa, and Penna and Dudley.

To add a local drawing card to the field of eight two-man teams, sportswriters from the local newspapers selected Les Bolstad, then the head pro at Minneapolis Golf Club, and Joe Coria, the head pro at Highland Park Golf Course in St. Paul, to compete as a team. They might have seemed like an afterthought compared to the touring pros, but Bolstad and Coria would be a big part of the story at the 1944 Invitational.

Shortly before the tournament was to begin, Dudley was forced to withdraw. The future head pro at Augusta National Golf Club would not be missed, however; Golden Valley landed a more than adequate replacement: Ben Hogan.

Lieutenant Hogan was training as a flight instructor in his home town of Fort Worth, and had played his first tournament in eighteen months the previous weekend, losing in an eighteen-hole Monday playoff at the Chicago Victory Open to McSpaden, the tour's leading money winner at the time. Hogan had practiced at his base and played some weekend golf, but his war duties had taken the polish off the game he'd developed in 1940, 1941 and 1942, when he'd been the PGA Tour's leading money winner.

Ben Hogan at Golden Valley
Courtesy: Paul Hardt

The major tasks of getting the Club ready for the event fell to Statt and Cooper, who arranged for fifty soldiers and sailors to assist in marshaling, and lined up local Boy Scout troops to help park cars in exchange for thirty-five dollars in equipment. Statt arranged for telephones and a trunk line for the press and others to use.

The excitement began Tuesday when some of the pros played a practice round. Even though persistent rains had the course playing long, Nelson and McSpaden looked poised to win the one that got away the previous year, warming up with a best-ball 65. Harbert was back to overpowering the course, missing a double-eagle two on the 524-yard par-five eighteenth hole by a couple of inches. Hogan stuck to the range, trying to straighten out the woods that were consistently off-line in Chicago.

Columnist George A. Barton of the *Minneapolis Morning Tribune* called it "far and away the most important golf tourney held in Minneapolis since Bobby Jones won the National Open at Interlachen in 1930 ... Old Man Par is in for an awful pasting and golf enthusiasts will witness the finest golfing staged in these parts since Jones, Walter Hagen and all other stars of amateur and professional ranks took Interlachen's difficult course apart with their sensational shooting fourteen years ago."

The prediction came true. Nelson and McSpaden picked up where they left off in 1943, firing a record twelve-under 61 to beat Harbert and Turnesa's 65. Unfortunately, the weather once again failed to cooperate – or, as the Tribune's Swanson put it, "records spattered around the premises like the persistent rain that has become the event's unrelenting theme song."

McSpaden was eight under par on his own ball over the nine-hole stretch from the fifth through fourteenth holes. He shot a 66 despite putting two balls out of bounds on the first hole (the Golden Valley Invitational was playing OB as a distance penalty only, instead of the normal USGA rule of a two-shot stroke-and-distance penalty.) The Nelson-McSpaden team was tied for first at +4 with Kaiser and Hamilton; three back were Hogan and Penna, who trailed most of their match to Cooper and Vines. As the rain pelted the foursome on the eighteenth green, Penna sank a forty-footer for birdie to win the match one-up.

"The rain, after threatening weather in keeping with last year's dismal starter, caught up with most of the boys at the nine-hole turn, never later than the twelfth," wrote Swanson. "But the boys played right through it, in shirtsleeves – and in record-making tempo – and the galleries stayed to the last. Those people who followed their favorites to the finish should be given medals."

Bolstad and Coria dropped their first match on Thursday to Kaiser and Hamilton, and then had to face the Nelson-McSpaden and Hogan-Penna teams Friday. The local pair combined for a 65 to gain a surprising tie against Nelson and McSpaden, who were tied for the lead at +5 after the second day; and they lost their afternoon match to Hogan-Penna by three.

"They try too hard," Penna said of the Bolstad-Coria team. "They should relax, even though they are trying so hard to make good before the home folks." Hogan had his own home-town follower to impress: his wife Valerie, according to the Tribune, "a pretty little southern lady with a fetching accent, appeared for the first time and watched her famous Air Corps husband from time to time."

In what the Tribune called "perfect weather," McSpaden and Nelson pushed their total to +14 after Saturday's play, but their five-hole lead was overshadowed by the amazing round shot by Bolstad and Coria. The local pair set a professional best-ball record with a 59, fourteen under par on the par-73 Golden Valley course. They finished with a back-nine 28 to stomp the Harbert-Turnesa team by seven holes.

"By no stretch of the imagination must it be stated that Bolstad and Coria survived to their record performance through the magic of a putter," Swanson wrote in the Tribune.

1943 Golden Valley Invitational Program
Courtesy: GVGCC

"They were good all the way from tee-to-green, and terrific from there in."

Coria made a thirty-footer on the first hole for an eagle; Bolstad birdied the second hole from thirty feet; Coria sank a fifteen-footer for birdie on four; both of their short birdie putts were conceded on six; Bolstad made a deuce on the par-three eighth; and the duo was six under at the turn. On the back nine, Coria started with ten- and fifteen-foot birdie putts on holes ten and eleven; both made gimme birdies on the par-five thirteenth; Coria birdied from twenty-five feet below the hole on fourteen; Bolstad made birdie putts from twenty feet above the hole on fifteen and thirty feet on sixteen; Coria birdied the par-three seventeenth from twenty-five feet while Bolstad waited to hit a short birdie putt of his own; and Bolstad finished the spectacular round with a birdie on the par-five eighteenth. "I hit it as hard as any shot I ever made," he said of his second shot to eighteen, which finished just off the green. He knocked his chip stiff.

On most holes, the partner closer to the hole putted first, and if he missed, the other would then putt. That happened so rarely, however, that Bolstad had putted just six times through the first twelve holes. "No use putting when Joe already has his birdie or eagle," Bolstad said. "I'd rather save my concentration for the final three rounds." Combined, they had just twenty-one putts all day.

1944 Golden Valley Invitational Program
Courtesy: GVGCC

The Bolstad-Coria scorecard was auctioned off the next day, and was purchased for $2,650 in war bonds by Golden Valley member Otto Hardt. He had every participant sign the scorecard.

Bolstad and Coria cooled off in the afternoon – perhaps partially due to Coria developing a blister on his finger that had to be taped between rounds. They lost to Cooper and Vines by two, leaving them at -2 for the tournament, twelve behind Nelson and McSpaden.

By the end of the day Saturday, more spectators had watched the 1944 Invitational than had attended the entire event the previous year. Still, the attendance was not what the Golden Valley committee had hoped for: 500 on Wednesday, 900 Thursday, 1,200 Friday and 2,000 on a perfect Saturday. A crowd of 5,000 was anticipated for Sunday's finale, but, as might have been expected, rain marred the Sunday morning rounds before letting up for the afternoon matches. Two consecutive years of disappointing attendance made it clear that there would not be a third Golden Valley Invitational.

Bolstad, left, and Coria with their 59 scorecard
Courtesy: Minneapolis Morning Tribune

"All of these changes helped," Cameron said. "The raising of the dues meant more income and a higher caliber of members. The family membership changed the entire feeling around the Club, made possible the women's club, and made for more dining room and buffet patrons."

The one negative development was the failure of the Club's plan to sell enough stock to the members to retire the mortgage of $38,000. Instead, the Club refinanced its mortgage, taking out a new $30,000 loan over ten years.

The Club did have enough money to buy a parcel of tax-delinquent land on the north boundary of the property. Between 1946 and 1947, the Club ended up buying seventy-six lots for a total of $4,476.82, due to fears that the Highway Department would run Olson Memorial Highway through part of the golf course. The Highway Department chose a different road alignment, however, leaving the golf course untouched. The purchase of those lots, however, allowed the eighth hole to be lengthened and a new green built on the former location of the ninth tee. In addition, a pond was dug in the eighth fairway to help drain the often soggy seventh fairway.

Membership was on the upswing; there was talk going into 1946 that a limit on members would have to be discussed once the total reached 275. In addition, the Club extended honorary memberships to Patty Berg and Bea Barrett Altmeyer, the two best women golfers in Minnesota. Joe Coria, having left his job as head pro at Highland Park, also became a member in 1946. That summer, Bernadine Rosenthal of Midland Hills defeated Jean Ann Perrine of Interlachen by ten shots to win the Women's Amateur stroke play championship at Golden Valley.

In a letter to Cameron, Fred Storms proposed that all caddie fees should be paid through the golf shop, with no tipping allowed. To improve caddie performance, Storms suggested that a prize of "a new [school] outfit" should be offered to the caddie earning the greatest number of merit marks. The second-place caddie would get a new hat and shoes, or new books and school supplies. The third-place caddie would receive whichever prize the second-place caddie turned down.

Guy Masters became Club president in 1947, taking over for Cameron, who summed up the progress made during his six years as president:

"Now when a member brings his family or a guest to the Club he enters the grounds through an attractive stone gateway entrance, drives his car over hard surface roads and parks his car in the nicely appointed roomy parking space. The Club house has been converted from a dilapidated or run-down shelter to a completely renovated and redecorated building."

Cameron cited new steel supports that reinforced the building, the newly shingled roof, new insulation, a new heating plant for year-round operation, a "greatly improved" locker room, a new card room, a service bar, walk-in refrigeration, flower gardens, repaired and painted fences, six new foot bridges and two new service bridges across Bassett Creek.

Early that winter, the Club was contacted by the PGA to see if there was interest in hosting another Invitational, but Invitational chairman Fred Storms objected to any tournament being held until financial backing was assured by the community. A committee was formed to canvas the situation, and evidently found little community support. The St. Paul Open was back on the PGA schedule, precluding the need for another pro event in the Twin Cities.

Harold Sieg

Until Harold Sieg was hired as Golden Valley's head pro in 1947, the longest any pro had held that job was nine years by Otis George (1919 to 1928). Prior to Sieg's arrival, there had been a series of short stints served by Pat Sawyer (1936-1937), Ray Keller (1938-1940), Harry Cooper (1941-1944) and Les Bolstad (1945-1946).

Though he was not a PGA tour star like Cooper or a Minnesota golf legend like Sawyer or Bolstad, Sieg was a solid, hard-working professional who held the job for fifteen years. He is still remembered as a fine teacher and a friendly presence in the golf shop.

Sieg learned club-making from a Scottish pro in Wichita, Kansas, and brought that skill with him to Minnesota, where he first worked at Northwood Country Club in St. Paul before taking a job in Minot, North Dakota.

Harold Sieg
Courtesy: GVGCC

Sieg learned from English pro Henry Cotton, a three-time winner of the Open Championship in Great Britain. At Golden Valley, Sieg gave free golf lessons to women each Tuesday morning. "As I recall, there were about fifteen women golfers when I came to Golden Valley, and about 160 when I left," Sieg said in later years.

Upon being named Golden Valley's pro, Sieg proposed a 10 x 30 addition to the golf shop to store members' clubs and provide additional sales space. In exchange, he offered to pay an additional twenty-five dollars per month shop rent. The Board approved the $1,500 project, and Sieg ultimately built four hundred club storage racks himself. His other innovations included building a practice tee shack, introducing motorized golf carts, promoting winter sports by offering a line of winter sports clothing and equipment, and enlarging the skating rink.

Sieg instituted a training school for caddies and hired a local coach to be the caddiemaster. "We had the finest set of caddies in the U.S.," Sieg once said as he looked back over his career.

"I remember Harold was a Sam Snead kind of guy, with a brimmed hat like Snead," said Rick Rendahl, who was a junior member in the nineteen-fifties. "He loved to hit golf balls, and was a very good teacher. He was gregarious to all the members, of course. He was just terrific. On Saturday and Sunday mornings he was on the first tee, and nobody left the first tee without having a tip to work on. He had a love for the game."

According to Don Fink, who worked for Sieg as an assistant from 1960 to 1963, Sieg didn't play a lot of golf. "I don't ever remember him going out and playing with the members," said Fink, who became Golden Valley's head pro in 1970. "If he did, it was very, very seldom. He had his friends and enemies like anybody did. He didn't pay a lot, but I probably wasn't worth a lot at that time."

"Harold Sieg was a classic," said John Sieff, who joined Golden Valley in 1953. "I can remember, I was at a golf tournament, and he heard my voice — we could tell each other without opening our eyes. Harold didn't play a lot at all, and he was kind of crabby at times. But he was a great guy, and very good teacher."

Sieg left Golden Valley after the 1963 season but continued to give lessons, including many years at Edinburgh USA Golf Course in Brooklyn Park. He died in 2006 at the age of ninety-six.

Jim Turnesa, Byron Nelson, Jug McSpaden, and Mike Turnesa at the 1943 Golden Valley Invitational
Courtesy: GVGCC

After two years at Golden Valley, both Bolstad and Iverson submitted their resignations in February 1947, and both were accepted, Bolstad's with "extreme reluctance and regret." The Board voted honorary memberships to Bolstad, Cameron and charter member Charles W. Sawyer.

Iverson was replaced by C.E. Chester. There was plenty of competition to replace Bolstad, who took a job coaching and teaching at the University of Minnesota course that would one day be named after him. Herbert Graffis of *Golfdom* magazine submitted a letter mentioning twenty potential candidates. Bolstad sent a letter to the Board recommending that they make their choice between Harold Sieg, Vernon "Red" Allen, Wally Ulrich and Lyle "Bud" Werring. Golden Valley chose Sieg, and got a keeper. He would be a fixture at Golden Valley for the next fifteen years. He was paid $300 per month on a twelve-month basis and received all net profits from the golf shop up to $5,400, with additional profits split between the Club and Sieg.

In 1947, Golden Valley Golf Club had three hundred golf members and a waiting list, yet money problems persisted. In his annual report, president Masters reported the Club was in a weak cash position, with a number of delinquent member accounts. The Board authorized Masters and Kunz to borrow against the Club's liquor stock as collateral, and voted that no more liquor was to be purchased until the existing stock was used up. The Club was also hurting in the pro shop, where Sieg had $3,600 in inventory, of which $2,300 was past due to suppliers. By January of 1948, the Club owed Sieg $2,600 because of insufficient funds in the treasury, and Sieg owed his creditors $4,000.

Paul Schmid said there was no use skimping on the golf course while pouring money into the clubhouse, which he described as being "in extremely bad condition," despite Cameron's glowing assessment of the building a year earlier. Masters reported that even the Club's slot machine revenue was down about $1,000 per month.

Dues were raised to two hundred dollars per year in 1948, but there still wasn't enough money to run the Club. In November the Board authorized an increase in the mortgage on the property from $15,600 to $30,000. At the shareholders meeting in January 1949, Masters reported that creeping inflation was leading to increased costs. The profits that had been anticipated to cover the $30,385.53 spent on capital improvements during 1946, 1947 and 1948 never materialized.

Clearly, something had to change.

The July 9, 1944 Minneapolis Morning Tribune reports on the final PGA Event held at Golden Valley

Courtesy: Minneapolis Morning Tribune

PART FOUR
THE SHRINERS TAKE OVER

In early December, Guy Masters announced that "the membership of the Club has reduced, in number, to a size which makes profitable operations of the Club almost impossible." It was the opinion of the Board that it could not reasonably anticipate profitable operations in the future under the present organizational set-up. The Board called for a shareholders meeting to request the authority to sell the Club.

At the special shareholders meeting on December 20, 1949, member C.H. Denesen and his guest Ralph Hegman, representing a group of members of the Zuhrah Temple of the Shrine in Minneapolis, said they had studied the feasibility of purchasing Golden Valley Golf Club. Though the Shriners would not have an offer ready for two weeks, the shareholders voted overwhelmingly – 516 shares to twenty-seven, or eighty-five percent in favor – to sell the property and assets of the Club for a price not less than the total amount of the principal balance, and the additional sum of $200,000.

The Shriners' first offer, made on January 13, 1950, was rejected because it lacked specifics of time and price. They were asked to present another offer; meanwhile, the Club split its stock into six hundred shares of non-voting Class A stock, and one thousand shares of Class B stock with voting rights. The current stockholders who held Class A stock could exchange each share for one and two-thirds shares of Class B stock. The exchanged Class A stock would be canceled.

With this increased liquidity and transferability of stock, the Golden Valley Golf Club was sold to the group of Shriners. The February 6, 1950 St. Paul Dispatch reported – somewhat inaccurately – that "The Zuhrah Temple of the Shrine bought Golden Valley Golf Course for $227,500. Present members can stay; all future members must belong to the Shrine. The Club is to be called Shriners Golden Valley Country Club."

Dairy owner Ray Ewald, leader of the group of ten Shriners who bought the Club, became the new president. Each member of the Club (golf and social) was required to own at least one of the one thousand shares of stock that were issued; each shareholder would have one vote, regardless of the amount of stock owned. Each share cost two hundred and fifty dollars and there was no initiation fee for the new members.

"They were fun Minneapolis business people, not all corporate," said Rick Rendahl, a future club president whose father joined Golden Valley in 1951. "There were a lot of small business people, though you couldn't prove that by what they've done to their businesses."

One of the new Club bylaws stated, "The membership of this corporation shall be reserved at all times to persons in good standing in the Ancient Arabic Order of Nobles of the Mystic Shrine." Yet there remained as many as fifty members of the old Club who were not Shriners. After much debate by the Board, it was finally decided to allow those members to stay, although they would not have voting rights. "They stayed, and were a big asset to the new Club," recalled Carl Jensen, who became Club president in 1959.

The new Board also debated whether to grant itself the power to assess members for improvements to the Club. The previous Board did not have that authority, which had necessitated the Club's incurring bank debt to cover costly expenditures. The Club seemed evenly split on the question, but ultimately chose to continue barring assessments. Jensen later said that decision caused "many a headache" for subsequent Boards.

Nevertheless, the new Club appeared to be an immediate success, gaining two hundred new members by mid-June of 1950. More members meant a need for an expanded and upgraded clubhouse, but there wasn't enough money. A $7,000 bank note with Northwestern National Bank was renewed, and two months later the Club paid off that loan with a new $12,000 private loan that gave the Club some much-needed working capital.

The financial gymnastics did not prevent Golden Valley from hosting the 1950 State Amateur championship. Ade Simonsen, later to become a Golden Valley member, but playing out of Minneapolis Golf Club at the time, defeated Al Clasen of Como Golf Course 10 & 8. Simonsen repeated the following year at Oak Ridge.

John Sieff joined Golden Valley Golf Club in 1953 as a full member. He was a Shriner and found Golden Valley convenient to his downtown job. It was also more enjoyable to play a less crowded private course than the public rounds he'd been playing at Westwood Hills, Hiawatha, Meadowbrook and Wirth.

"I was poor at the time, but they needed members," Sieff recalled "It was only two hundred and fifty dollars to join. The dues were twenty-five dollars a month. Golden Valley was just coming out of the doldrums and needed a lot. It had a very old clubhouse on the hill."

The first time Sieff saw Golden Valley was at the 1931 Trans-Mississippi tournament, when he was just a little boy. He remembers attending the Golden Valley Invitational with his neighbors. When he became a member, his primary goal was to make new friends. He was placed with members he didn't know, yet found them welcoming. The club became even friendlier as it made the transition from golf club to country club.

"I joined in 1953 with my brother John, who was four years older than me," recalled Al Yngve, who was twenty-four at the time, had just come home from the Korean War, and owned a drive-in restaurant in Golden Valley. "We were intermediate members. Our dad was a Shriner, and he bought three shares of stock. We didn't have to be Shriners, but later we joined the Shrine."

The golf course was difficult and very dry in the hot summer months, Yngve said. "The irrigation system wasn't that good. We had above-ground sprinklers that were moved around. The roughs died out in August." As the membership increased and overhead was reduced, the Club built up enough cash reserves to install a much needed single-line irrigation system.

No one at the club wanted to go into debt to renovate the thirty-year-old clubhouse, and assessments were not an option, but a larger dining room was imperative, so ten dollar donations were sought from the members. Enough money was raised to do some limited remodeling, but the need for a new clubhouse was becoming more and more apparent.

The Board raised golf dues to $175, but the Club continued to attract new members and gain revenue. President Ewald told the membership at the annual meeting in January 1954 that the Club needed just twenty more stock subscriptions to have enough cash to pay off its mortgage. To great applause and cheers, twenty-three members immediately stood and subscribed for the additional shares. A gala mortgage burning party was held on June 12, 1954.

> **TO GOLDEN VALLEY CLUB MEMBERS:**
>
> The year 1954 will be remembered as the year of the burning of the mortgage. This was accomplished after three short years, since Golden Valley became a golf and country club for Shriners.
>
> Enlargement of the already spacious facilities, for your convenience, will also become a reality in 1954.
>
> The Board of Directors joins me in wishing you a good game, enchanting weather, and a wonderful social season.
>
> **RAY C. EWALD**, *President*

Excerpt from 1954 Membership Roster
Courtesy: GVGCC

The following year, the question of a new clubhouse became top priority. A 1955 straw poll of the membership favored the building of a new $150,000 clubhouse over remodeling the old one, but a more detailed study of the issue the next year indicated that the cost would be substantially higher. In July 1956 the Board asked the membership for approval to take out a mortgage of $325,000 to build a 24,000 square foot clubhouse, and the measure was approved by a wide margin.

Before plans for the new clubhouse could be drawn up, the Club received a proposal from Baker Properties of Minneapolis to buy the Golden Valley Golf Club and convert it into 320 home lots, in exchange

Ray Ewald

The first president of the Shriner-owned Golden Valley Golf Club is remembered today for his humble rise from driving a milk wagon through the streets of Minneapolis to his position as co-owner of the city's most prosperous dairy. But Ray Ewald was far more than a dairyman. Though he worked in denim overalls with a team of horses as he sold milk in South Minneapolis throughout the 1920s, by the 1950s he was a political insider who had the ear of one of America's most powerful men.

Ray Ewald
Courtesy: GVGCC

The Ewald dairy was founded by Chris Ewald, the oldest son of the widowed Moa Ewald, who had come from Denmark to settle on a small farm at the intersection of 45th Street and 28th Avenue South in Minneapolis. When Chris was fourteen, he landed a job on a milk route, and purchased that route in 1886. Chris delivered the milk and herded the cattle with his nine-year-old brother, John.

Chris Ewald and his wife Gertine Hanson had eight daughters and four sons, including Ray, who was born in 1900. To accommodate his expanding business, Ewald leased the 700-acre McNair Farm in Golden Valley, now the site of Theodore Wirth Park, for one dollar per acre. After the Minneapolis Park Board bought the land around their home near Lake Hiawatha in 1911, Chris and John herded their cattle twelve miles to the McNair Farm, where they made their new home. Chris and his oldest son Robert ran the farm and younger sons Ray and Dewey delivered the milk. Chris built his first milk production plant across the street from the farm, on five acres he purchased in 1917.

In 1923, the Ewalds moved off the farm, choosing to buy the milk they processed instead of raising their own dairy cattle. The core of their business was milk delivery, powered until 1930 by horses, which were purchased for one hundred dollars a head and typically pulled a wagon for a dozen years. Modernization came in 1930 when Ewald Dairy bought a fleet of trucks; at its peak, Ewald's received milk from sixty-one farms and used 120 delivery trucks.

The business continued to grow and prosper after Chris died in 1938 and Ray and Dewey Ewald took over. During the nineteen-fifties, Ewald's had five hundred employees who handled one out of every three home delivery customers in the entire Minneapolis market.

A longtime Golden Valley member, Ray Ewald was on the reformed Board of Directors when the Club came out of receivership in 1940, and became the first Shriner president of the Golden Valley Golf Club ten years later. He was also a close friend of then-Senator Hubert Humphrey.

Ewald grew up in south Minneapolis next door to Luther Youngdahl, who went on to become an enormously popular Republican governor of Minnesota from 1947 to 1951. Ewald met Humphrey when Ewald was serving on the Minneapolis planning commission and the future Vice-president of the United States was mayor of the city. Ewald didn't have much use for Humphrey at first, describing him as a "young blabbermouth," according to Humphrey biographer Carl Solberg. But Ewald became impressed with the way Humphrey was always able to solve problems and get people to work together. He began contributing money to Humphrey's campaigns, and would frequently pick him up at the airport in his Cadillac.

In 1953 Humphrey rented Ewald's summer cottage on the shore of Waverly Lake, and became so comfortable there he bought six adjoining lots from Ewald, on which he built his permanent home. That sale would become a political issue fifteen years later during Humphrey's run for president; the Chicago Tribune reported that there was never a recorded purchase of the property, and that Ewald had given the lots to Humphrey at a time when the Ewald Dairy was going through an anti-trust action over alleged price-fixing. Humphrey labeled the report "bunk."

Ray and Dewey Ewald
Courtesy: GVGCC

Ewald played a role in his friend Luther Youngdahl's future, as well. Youngdahl had confided to Ewald that he would like a federal judgeship; Ewald passed the information on to Humphrey, who in turn gave it to President Harry Truman, hoping to take the unbeatable Youngdahl out of elective politics in Minnesota. When a judgeship opened up, Truman crossed party lines to give it to Youngdahl.

A devoted Shriner as well as a devoted member of the Club, Ewald's fondest dream was to have the Golden Valley Golf Club also serve as the site of a new Zuhrah Temple, which needed to relocate. He had in mind a plot of high ground immediately next to the clubhouse as he wrote in the April 1959 club newsletter:

> "On this ground could be built a Temple situated as few Temples are situated in this Country," Ewald wrote in the April 1959 club newsletter. "A temple, built along the lines of a Mosque, would complement our own club house and surely our club house would complement such a Temple. The grounds surrounding the Temple would not be more than fifteen minutes from any point in the Minneapolis business district, and a Shriner attending the Temple would be in the clean, country air of Golden Valley in the matter of minutes."
>
> "There could be an adequate, underground passage from the Temple to our club house, and the dining room facilities could be made available to Zuhrah Temple, for their various functions. The Zuhrah ladies could take advantage of our dining room and grill facilities. It would make the perfect set up for the ladies, when their husbands or sweethearts are at the Temple for Shrine activities."
>
> "If Zuhrah Temple does come to Golden Valley, there will be no need to ever look for a new location, for Golden Valley will endure as long as Shriners want it to. The rolling ground, the winding creek, that are Golden Valley, and which bring so much joy to all of us, would bring the same joy to Zuhrah Temple. There is no place that quite matches its beauty. It is my belief and the fondest dream of our finest Board of Directors, that the present Board of Directors will bring to reality the moving of Zuhrah Temple to Golden Valley. When that day comes, then the rolling hills that are Golden Valley, will seem more lush to us all, simply because the Shrine that is our Shrine, will be in Golden Valley. It can be done, so-o-o-o let's do it. This can be a great thing for both Golden Valley and Zuhrah Temple. Let's explore the possibilities to the fullest extent."

It may have been explored, but nothing came of Ewald's proposal. Ewald died in 1969, a year after his friend Hubert Humphrey lost his race for President of the United States to Richard Nixon.

Groundbreaking for the new clubhouse
Courtesy: GVGCC

for a new clubhouse and golf course at a location near Hamel, Minnesota. After studying the proposal, the Board turned it down, and went ahead with its plans. On March 5, 1957, the Board accepted a new clubhouse design submitted by member Clair Armstrong of the architectural firm of Armstrong and Schlichting. One of the strongest advocates for the new clubhouse was president Paul Johnson, who had joined the Club in 1927 and was also Potentate of Zuhrah Temple in 1950 when the Shriners purchased Golden Valley.

"The original plans called for a rejuvenation of the old clubhouse," Johnson told the members. "However, upon investigation, we discovered it would be impractical due to the age and condition of our present structure. At a meeting of the members, your Board of Directors was authorized to go ahead with plans for a new clubhouse. The new building will be located adjacent to the present site. We will utilize the property which is now being used as a drive and garden. We shall continue to use the old clubhouse until our new club is ready for occupancy. This will be another of our dreams come true."

Once the plans were tweaked and approved, the Board presented the following financing plan: The Club would borrow a sum not to exceed $475,000 for a new clubhouse and furnishing; encumber the assets of the corporation, not exceeding $395,000; and sell fifty-four lots of Club property north of the golf course. Those lots eventually netted the club $16,200.

The size of the clubhouse was slightly reduced after construction bids came in higher than estimated, and on May 16, 1957, a groundbreaking ceremony was held. The photo on the cover of the June issue of Golden Valley Golf Club News captured the moment: Ray Ewald directing the spade work of President Paul Johnson and Mayors Eric Hoyer of Minneapolis and Carl Nadasdy of Golden Valley.

"As you will observe by the pictures at the bottom of this page, the excavators are making progress," read a caption in that month's issue. "The huge pit you see is the area formerly used as our garden and driveway. Eventually the entire old clubhouse will be removed and the hill surrounding it. This will be the entrance to the new clubhouse. It will be impossible to erect the entrance until the old structure has been removed."

It was also necessary to move the location of the first tee closer to the road in order to make room for the handling and storage of materials. The new tee created a slight dog-leg and temporarily turned the hole into a par four. "To some of us plagued by the out-of-bounds hazard on this hole, this could prove to be a boon," said golf chairman Art Philip.

Members were charged an additional five dollars per month to cover the costs of some changes to the original plan, including an enlargement of the porch area, a concrete base for the cart storage area and furnishings for the grill. Construction by the Dean L. Witcher Company went quickly, and by February 1958 the Grille Room was opened for limited service.

It was a modern-looking one story building with a brick exterior and white stone chip roofing. The lower level housed the men's and women's locker rooms, shower rooms, the pro shop and a cart storage area below the patio. The lounge was located off the main entrance on the upper level, with a grill room and bar adjacent to that. The main dining room was capable of seating five hundred, and it opened to a large screened porch and terrace overlooking the first tee. The official grand opening of the new clubhouse was held over three nights May 2-4. Each night was a sell-out.

By the spring of 1958 the golf membership limit had been reached and a waiting list was established. The course was busy, with over 26,500 rounds played in 1959. Dues were $250 for men, an additional fifty dollars for the wife of a golf member, $125 for a single woman or wife of a social member, and sixty dollars additional for a family membership. The golf course underwent a new round of changes, described by new superintendent Frank Anderson in the Club newsletter:

"We felt that cutting down some of the severe mounds around some of the greens would not spoil the appearance of the greens, and would make maintenance much easier, because they require hand work," Anderson wrote. *The club also believed, to the consternation of later memberships, that this would "modernize" Tillinghast's course.*

"The chocolate drop [mounds] were eliminated and many deep traps at greenside were partially or completely filled in," Harold Sieg recalled. *"Numbers four, six and twelve come to mind. There was other easing. Greens at numbers three, ten, eleven, thirteen and seventeen were enlarged and several tees were relocated."*

Eliminating chocolate drop mounds like these behind the 2nd green were part of the Club's modernization efforts in the late fifties.
Courtesy: GVGCC

There were specific changes to several holes. When the USGA increased the minimum length of a par-five hole to 471 yards, Golden Valley's first and thirteenth holes officially became par-fours. The location of the first tee was moved closer to the road and farther back, adding twenty-eight yards to what was now a 491-yard par-five. The new angle for the tee shot played away from the out-of-bounds, and a row of trees was planted along the road.

The thirteenth hole was increased in length from 458 yards to 473 yards by building a new tee. The green committee believed the new tee lengthened the hole even further than the scorecard would show because many drives which previously landed on or over the top of the hill would now hit into the upslope. The same conditions affected the second shot from that location, leaving more blind shots to the green. In addition, a new bunker was added to the ninth fairway, a new refreshment stand/rain shelter with rest rooms was built behind the tenth tee, new sand was put in all the bunkers, and a new fence was built surrounding the course.

Al Yngve remembered what the bunkers were like before some were filled in during the late 1950s. "I took a lesson from Harold Sieg on how to get out of the bunkers," Yngve said. "They were so steep I had to get a special club. I bought a Kroydon wedge with a big flange and opened it up wide, swung hard and the ball popped out and onto the green. When they re-did them [in 1998], I went on E-Bay to look for a Kroydon wedge again, and I found one."

The best Golden Valley players at the time were Ted Hammerlund, who won two club championships, and Ted McFarlane, who reached the quarterfinals of the State Amateur in 1952 & 1955. The best woman player was Millie Bolstad, wife of the club's former pro. She won club championships in 1952, 1953, 1955 and 1956. When the Women's State Amateur came to Golden Valley in 1955 and 1959, Bev Vanstrum representing the University of Minnesota Golf Course (in '55) and Stillwater Country Club (in '59) won both events.

The most heartwarming event at Golden Valley in 1956 was former member and head pro, Pat Sawyer, returning to the Club to win the State Open with a three-under-par 216 at age forty-three, beating Ade Simonsen of Minneapolis Golf Club by one shot. They both shot a final-round 68, the low rounds of the tournament.

The social life of the club included businessmen's luncheons with guest speakers on Thursdays; bingo nights on those evenings with cash prizes and a one hundred dollar door prize; Sunday family dinners and winter bowling leagues at area lanes. There were also numerous theme parties: Mexican Fiesta, Lobster Bake, Speak-Easy Daze (with WCCO radio vocalist Tony Grise and his Hot Shot Rhythm Makers), Oriental (with Japanese dancers and Willie Peterson's Orchestra featuring WCCO's Jean Arland at the organ), Night in Paris, New Orleans, Las Vegas, Good Ol' Summertime, Aquatennial Showboat, Hawaiian, Western and Monte Carlo. In 1959 the club responded to many requests for a "name" band and booked Sammy Kaye and his Orchestra, veterans of the big band era. The dinner-dance was a sell-out, prompting the club to pose this question to its members: "How about trying to get Guy Lombardo – or a repeat on Sammy Kaye?" They would later successfully host the Wayne King and Woody Herman orchestras.

Club manager Bill Bell organized dancing lessons ("All the popular dances including the Rhumba, Mamba and Cha-Cha.") on Friday nights, taught by Dave and Sally LaVay, the dance instructors on the KSTP show "High Five." They also taught teenage dance lessons, including "Rock 'n' Roll," "Calypso" and "The Blues."

Bruce Smith, whose parents joined the Club in 1951, has fond memories of those days: "Back then we used to have a junior member dance party with the clubs in town like Woodhill, Minikahda, maybe Wayzata – the boys stand on one side, a disc jockey, and the girls standing on the other side."

The teen parties tended to feature safe, sedate music from their parents' era – bands like Doc Evans' Dixieland Band and Roger Eker's ten-piece Rhythm Ramblers. At the 1958 teen holiday party, however, somebody decided to push the boundaries. It was described in the Club newsletter: "The kind of a party any teenager would dream about. It was held in the main dining room with a live orchestra. This orchestra was really something special. What we mean is – they were a young group called The Sonics [a local rock 'n' roll group from Robbinsdale High School] and they had the beat for the type of dancing modern teenagers understand."

A sleigh ride and sock hop on Feb. 12, 1960, featured WDGY disc jockey Stanley Mack. The newsletter announcement: "All you cats, calves and kittens blow your jets but don't be a square or get flipped, and if you've got smog in the noggin be sure to put this affair on the front burner and make the club like Antsville."

A decade earlier, Golden Valley Golf Club had begun its transition away from what former President Cameron had called a "stag" club, but with the post-war baby boom now in full force, it became a priority for most clubs to provide other recreation activities to attract and keep members with children and teens. Club leaders decided a swimming pool would be the most effective enticement to those families.

It turned out to be a hard sell to the membership.

In early 1959 President Carl Jensen sent out a questionnaire to gauge the membership's interest in building a pool and tennis courts. A solid majority opposed the idea – 250 for, 316 against – but the comments were split on both sides, and Jensen pointed out that forty of the "no" votes were qualified by statements of "Not at present" or "reduce our present debt first," etc. Some other replies: "At least something for the social member to do. You can't eat all the time"; "Very strong for it. Get it ready by Memorial Day. Borrow money if necessary"; "Excellent. More members would join"; "Too old to use it"; "By all means, but let users pay for upkeep."

Two more comments: "As a result of lack of participation from social members we have been forced to allow use from outside organizations, discouraging our own members from using these facilities. Unless something is done we will probably lose more and more members to other clubs"; followed by, "Ridiculous."

One comment succinctly summed up the Board's reasoning for pushing the idea: "My husband plays golf only once in seven to ten days, because he feels guilty about leaving the rest of the family home in his limited free time. If there were a pool, he would probably play twice a week, and we would consume a family total of about six lunches and eight dinners per week in summer instead of our average of one lunch and two or three dinners, since we would not only come oftener, but also bring the children. Not to mention the liquor and soft drinks, etc. At present, the club is largely benefiting only one family member, and as our children grow up, the expense would begin to seem too one-sided to maintain. We have already joined one pool club, and may later transfer both memberships to a golf and pool club if G.V. doesn't keep up with other clubs."

In light of the opposition, the Board voted to table the issue, but it was back the following year. At the annual meeting of December 1959, the Board presented a proposal for a package of improvements totaling an estimated $200,000, including $90,000 for a swimming pool and $15,000 for two tennis courts and fences. To fund the construction, the Board proposed to change the rules to allow member assessments; the rest would be borrowed. The assessment measure was defeated 273-201; the pool was defeated 304 to 177, although the membership expressed approval for an enlargement of the grill room and an upgrade to the faulty air conditioning system. In June 1960 the Board restructured the proposal to include an expansion of the dining room, which was already considered inadequate. Then, in November, the swimming pool supporters turned on the hard sell with a letter in the club newsletter, "submitted by a group of members who are interested in the addition of a swimming pool at the Club. Names available upon request to the management":

"Gentlemen: Since the swimming pool proposal was defeated in a vote a year ago, there seems to have been a change in opinion. It was located some distance from the clubhouse, and presented as a package deal with tennis courts and many members wanted the pool but not the courts. Also there was considerable confusion about the method of financing and also confusion about the method of voting.

"There should be no question that eventually we must have a pool at our club because already every first rate golf club in the country has a swimming pool. Most Twin Cities clubs have pools or are in the process of building one. Primarily we need a pool now to attract new young Shriners to become social members at GVGC, otherwise these prospective members will join other clubs with pool facilities ... We may lose some of our best members to other clubs. Three dollars per month added to the five dollars per month for the club expansion should be enough to build an adequate pool.

"We feel the ideal location for a pool would be immediately to the West and adjacent to the clubhouse with a terrace off of the grill and Valley View rooms overlooking the pool. This location would not interfere with

Harold Van Every

Harold "Hal" Van Every was the last living connection to Golden Valley's turbulent, storied early days, and a hero in anyone's book.

Van Every was born in 1918 in Minnetonka Beach and started working at age eight, first delivering newspapers, then caddying at the nearby Lafayette Club and working as a lifeguard. He helped lead the Wayzata High School football and basketball teams to several Lake Conference Championships. He was a star football player for the University of Minnesota Golden Gophers (1937-1939), playing both halfback and defensive back on two Big Ten championship teams in 1937 and 1938 under coach Bernie Bierman. He set the single-season team record for interceptions with eight, and was voted the team's most valuable player in 1939, a season in which he lead the Gophers in rushing with 733 yards. He also lettered one year in basketball.

His greatest game came in 1938 against arch-rival Michigan, just days after being released from the hospital for treatment of a ruptured kidney. With the Gophers trailing 6-0 in the fourth quarter, Van Every recovered a fumble by Michigan's All-American halfback Tom Harmon. Van Every then threw the game-winning touchdown pass, called "one of the most sensational and important plays ever staged at Memorial Stadium" by the Minneapolis Tribune, thrilling the homecoming crowd of 56,000 and securing the Little Brown Jug for Minnesota.

Harold Van Every
Courtesy: Rick Shefchik

Curly Lambeau, coach and general manager of the defending NFL champion Green Bay Packers, selected Van Every ninth overall in the 1940 NFL draft. He signed a $3,500 contract as a running back, defensive back and punter. He used part of his rookie salary to buy his mother a washing machine; with his second season's salary, he had hot water supplied to his parent's upstairs bathroom. Van Every rarely drank alcohol or went to taverns. To relax, he played the piano in the hotel lobby while his teammates were out carousing.

Van Every led the 10-1 Packers with three interceptions in 1941, returning one for a ninety-one-yard touchdown, but the team lost the Western Conference finals 33-14 to the Chicago Bears. Van Every scored the last touchdown of the game, and the last of his career, on a ten-yard pass from Cecil Isbell.

A week before the Bears game, Japan attacked Pearl Harbor. Van Every joined the Army Air Corps in 1942 and received his pilot training in Sacramento, California. He married his wife, Drexel Kay Weck of Slayton, Minnesota, in Carson City, Nevada, on July 27, 1942. After returning to duty, he was sent to England's Rattlesden Air Base in 1941 to pilot a B-17 bomber.

In May 1944, Van Every's plane was hit by anti-aircraft fire. He and his crew of nine parachuted out of their aircraft; Van Every landed on the roof of a house, and severely injured his back on a fence while jumping to the ground. He tried to escape the German troops but was captured in nearby woods, and spent a year in Stalag Luft III in Sagan, Germany, along with approximately 10,000 American and British air troops.

While imprisoned, Van Every lost fifty pounds from his 6-foot-1, two hundred pound frame. His Packers won their sixth NFL championship in December 1944, but Van Every would not find out about it until several months later.

Back home, his wife Drexel attended the 1944 Golden Valley Invitational in July. She told a reporter at the event that she wrote letters to Harold each day – forty-seven of them to that point – but since they couldn't be mailed, she was saving them for his return.

"It was pretty tough without my wife and football," Van Every told a Milwaukee newspaper reporter in 2006. "I was lucky to get out of there and make it back home. I was in good shape physically, except for my back. It was pretty rough going."

Van Every kept a journal of his life in captivity: cold, overcrowded barracks with twelve men to a room, a week-long march in sub-zero temperatures, riding in a box car with ravaged prisoners to a new, vermin-infested camp in Nuremberg, eating "green death" soup and worm-infested vegetables. "The Red Cross food packages saved us," he said.

Van Every and his fellow prisoners were freed on April 29, 1945, by General George Patton's troops. After returning to the United States, Lambeau asked him if he could resume his football career, but Van Every's back injury ruled out a return to the gridiron.

Finished with football and fighting, Van Every raised a family, built a successful career in the Minneapolis insurance business, and gave much of his spare time to community service. He took leading roles with Big Brothers and YMCA Camp Warren, and joined the Zuhrah Temple of the Shrine. Sports Illustrated honored him in 1964 with the Silver Anniversary All-America award for his community work. In 1994 he was inducted into the University of Minnesota Athletics Hall of Fame.

He underwent back surgery four times and wore a back brace for more than fifty years. That did not keep him from fishing, tennis and golf, however. He played tennis twice a week until he was eighty and played golf at Golden Valley three times a week. He won the Golden Valley Senior Club Championship in 1987 and shot his age when he was eighty-six. He continued to play golf – and the piano – until his death at age eighty-nine in 2007.

"You'd never guess what he had achieved in his life by talking to him," said his son, Dale Van Every, of Minneapolis. "What made him so great is that he didn't know he was so great."

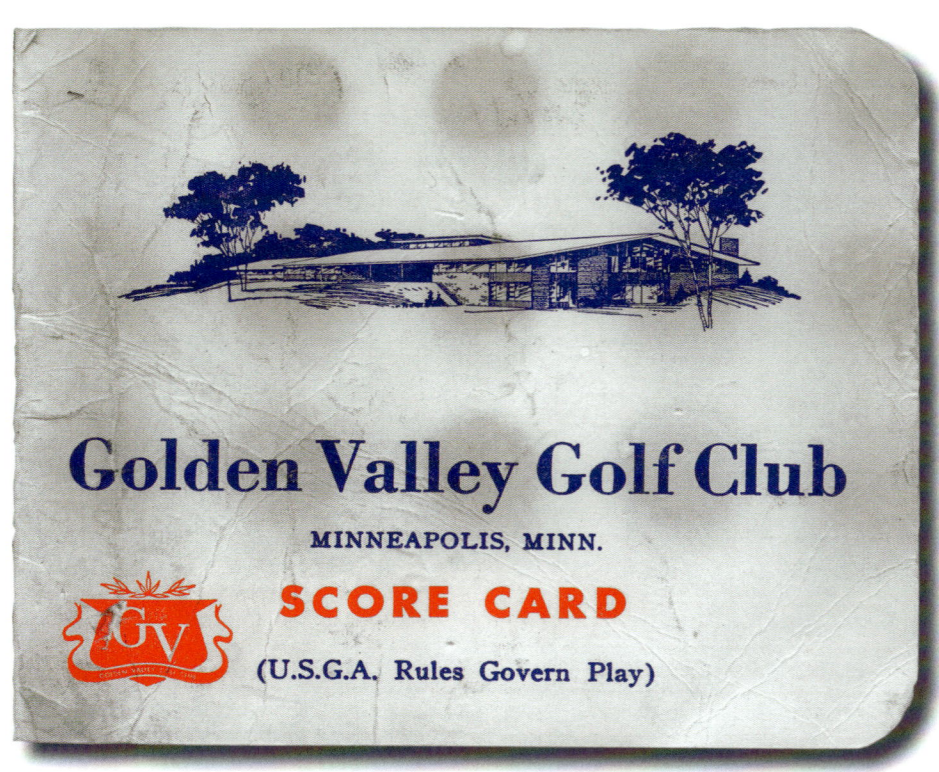

Club Scorecard from the late '60s
Courtesy: GVGCC

the script. We always got the presidents and past presidents into something, a skit or song and dance. It was so wonderful. This was one thing where the golfers and diners and the pool people got together. It didn't matter who did what. This is how they got to know each other. They loved it."

The golfers held the spotlight in 1967, when the State Amateur Championship returned to Golden Valley. That was the year the Minnesota Golf Association permanently switched the Amateur to a stroke-play format. Robert Magie III of Northland Country Club in Duluth won the seventy-two-hole event, shooting two-under-par 290. No one broke 70 on the par 73 course. Two years later, Jody Gumlia of Crookston won the Women's State Amateur match play championship 1-up over Joan Garvin of Minnesota Valley at Golden Valley. Gumlia defeated future U.S. Women's Open winner Jerilyn Britz of Worthington 1-up in the semis.

Costs rose faster than revenue by the end of the decade. In response, the Club enforced the payment of delinquent accounts, stopped publishing its newsletter, reduced the number of employees and cut the number of parties to four or five per year. With those measures, finances stabilized well enough for the club to undertake a few clubhouse improvement projects, including the construction of a storage area under the patio, weatherizing the porch off the men's card room, and extending a canopy over the front entrance.

The Club experienced another setback when an explosion and fire destroyed the basement of the storage building in 1970, taking with it all the non-active Club records. The few documents that remain were turned in by members who had copies in their personal files.

The Board tried to raise money for repairs and improvements by selling ten-year maturity debentures worth one hundred dollars at seven percent interest, but members purchased only half of the $80,000 in debentures, so the plan was scrapped.

"With the advent of the Twins, the Vikings, outdoors being an option, snowmobiles, there were a lot more options, for any member, Shriner or other, to do other things," said Rick Rendahl, who became a Shriner so he could join the club in 1968. "The Shrine was a huge center for business and pleasure, but by the early seventies, people started going to the cabin more than they used to, and sporting events flourished. You saw more people wanting to join but didn't want to be Shriners."

The only feasible alternative to raising dues was to attract new members, and there was only one way to do that: Remove the requirement that a member had to belong to the Shrine or the Masons. The measure passed in 1971, along with changing the corporation's name to the Golden Valley Country Club.

"The membership numbers were suffering," recalled Al Yngve. "It brought us a lot of good, new young members. It became more of a family club, and that was fine with me. I don't think it bothered anybody."

"There was very little controversy, as I recall," Rendahl said.

"It was something that had to be done to enable us to recruit members," said Charles Hvass, who was club president in 1972. "It went hand-in-hand with building the pool and tennis courts to broaden the value for members and our recruiting efforts,"

Golden Valley Golf and Country Club Aerial Photograph: 2010
Looking eastward toward downtown
Courtesy: GVGCC

PART FIVE ~ COUNTRY CLUB

The change to a country club, open to all applicants, brought in a wave of new members, which in turn created a new set of physical needs for the Club. A capital program called Project 72 was created to complete the front entry canopy, renovate the card room and porch, enlarge the pro shop, remodel the women's locker room, build additional tennis courts and expand the cart and club storage area. The shareholders approved a $700,000 loan that would cover those costs and pay off the $360,000 mortgage. The energy crisis of the early seventies threw the club into financial peril once again, leading to more trying times for the club, according to Charles Coulter, who was president of the club in 1975. "There was a membership decline and refinancing was required in order to proceed with necessary renovations. The Boards during this period were constantly under great pressure to simply make ends meet."

In 1970, Don Fink returned to Golden Valley to replace Joe Sodd as head pro. Fink had worked as an assistant to Harold Sieg and then Sodd from 1960 to 1966, then took a head pro job at the Minnehaha Country Club in Sioux Falls, South Dakota.

The Minnesota State Amateur Championship returned to Golden Valley for the fifth time in 1972, and was won by University of Minnesota All-American Rick Ehrmanntraut, who shot a four-under par 215 for fifty-four holes.

Don Fink

Don Fink was the longest-serving head pro in the history of Golden Valley Golf and Country Club, from 1970 to 2001. Throw in the seven years he worked there as an assistant, and Fink devoted thirty-nine years of his life to serving the Club.

Longest Serving Head Pro, Don Fink
Courtesy: GVGCC

He and his wife Kathy were St. Paul through and through. He grew up on Rice Street, and attended St. Bernard's and Cretin; she went to Nativity and Our Lady of Peace High School. They met at a mixer at the Prom Ball Room on University Avenue. Fink was a baseball player in high school, but after a six-month stint in the Army, he became interested in golf. A friend of a friend got him a job at Midland Hills, where he worked for a year in 1959. In 1960 he was hired by Harold Sieg at Golden Valley Golf Club. He later worked for Sieg's successor Joe Sodd.

"It was not in my mind to be head pro here," Fink said after his retirement. "Once Harold left, and I worked for Joe, I started to think a little more about it."

There would be a detour, however. In 1967 he "got lucky" and was offered the job of head pro at the Minnehaha Country Club in Sioux Falls, South Dakota. "This is a bigger club as far as the Twin Cities goes," Fink said. "I can understand they wanted experience at someplace else. Minnehaha turned out fine. I replaced a school teacher, so I looked good to them. I enjoyed it. Sioux Falls is a great town. I wouldn't have left there if it hadn't been Golden Valley."

When Fink found out about the Golden Valley opening, he sent in his resume. He had a leg up on the other applicants: He and his wife were from the Twin Cities, he'd worked at the Club for seven years, he knew a lot of the members and the majority of them were still there.

"It's always been a great club for meeting people and getting games," Fink said. "Ninety percent of the time if you came out alone you'd find a group to play with. They were always good that way. We've had a lot of characters, and a lot of stories I wouldn't dare tell you. Some guys would call up Vegas – they knew some people who could get them a room, and all of the sudden they'd fly out there, call home and say they weren't coming home for dinner. Ninety-five percent of the members are great people. I always felt you needed a few of the others to appreciate them. I've made a lot of friends here. I still see them. Of course a lot of them are gone – some have passed, some have moved."

With club president Charlie Hvass, Fink helped revitalize a caddie program that remains strong into the club's second century, producing frequent Evans Scholars and providing young people with an opportunity to learn about the game of golf while they earn money.

Fink personally entered every score from every member while he was head pro. "We had a friend playing our course from Cincinnati, and he asked, 'What do you do about handicaps?'" said Rick Rendahl. "We turn our score in, and the pro enters every one of them. It's an honor system. He'd never heard of anybody doing that. Don was a stickler for rules and interpretations, and anything that got close to somebody taking advantage of the situation – people accused of not counting all the strokes – we had several members tossed out of the club because of stuff that happened that way. Being a pro, you've got to be fair."

Members described Fink as a patient, impartial arbiter who did not show favoritism to anyone, while remaining popular with a diverse membership.

For several years, Fink brought three Golden Valley players to an annual event at the TPC course in Dallas, hosted by Byron Nelson, called "11 Straight." It celebrated the 50th anniversary of Nelson's eleven straight wins on the PGA tour in 1945. The invitations went out to clubs where Nelson had worked and won tournaments. Fink said Nelson remembered Golden Valley from his win with Jug McSpaden in the 1944 Invitational. There was a dinner Sunday night prior to the first round, and on Monday night the participants took a half-hour bus ride to Nelson's house.

"They had a big tent set up where we had dinner, and you could go through his house at your leisure," Fink said. "Talk about memorabilia. It was all over the place. You could take pictures. He had a modest home, nothing elaborate, but that's the kind of guy he was. He was a classy guy. His second wife was there. She said she was learning how to walk when he was winning his tournaments.

"I went down there a few times, then I sent Henry [Orme]. The course was getting too long for me. The pros teed off twenty yards behind where the amateurs hit, and I'm not a long hitter. We finished tied for second or third the first year. All the guys that went, they loved it."

Though he played just fifteen to twenty rounds per year, Fink's low round at Golden Valley was a 67. Yet he had no illusions about his abilities. "I'm a hot dog player," he said. "You watch a golf tournament – Woods and Mickelson are coming up, lets watch them. McIlroy and Westwood – ooh, lets watch them. Who's coming here? Orme and Fink. Let's go get a hot dog."

"Don rarely played," said Rendahl. "When he retired, all of a sudden he got good again. Now they're all mad at him when he hits from the gold tees. He hits it straight – he's always hit it straight. He's an absolute treat to watch warm up. He goes to the range, hits every club in the bag, and hits them all straight. He's a great individual for the club – he's never forgotten anybody's name, ever. A guy told me, 'I ran into your old pro, he hadn't seen me in twenty-five years, but he picked me out of a crowd and told me a story.'"

The members demonstrated their respect and affection for their self-effacing pro by giving him a lifetime membership at his retirement party in 2001, attended by past Golden Valley pros Pat Sawyer, Harold Sieg and Joe Sodd. Like most retirees, Fink then began playing more golf.

"All the years he was a pro, I maybe played with him two or three times at most," said Christenson. "Now I've played with him many times. It's nice to see him enjoying retirement, for his own benefit and to us members. He has a nice game. We see him in a different capacity as participant rather than overseer, and that's nice for the membership."

"I probably didn't play with members as much as I should have, but I was running the caddie program, the shop – it gets to be a lot," he said. "I'm trying to make up for it now. It's fun – sometimes, I'll play with three guys who all hit it thirty yards beyond me, but we'll come in and sometimes I'll have the lowest score. It's a great game."

The initiation fee for new golf members was $1,500 in 1973, rose to $2,500 in 1975 and increased again to $3,500 by 1977. In 1977 a pond was dug to the right of the seventeenth green to handle runoff water from Golden Valley Road. It was a controversial issue – Charlie Hvass was concerned someone might fall in – but such decisions were made by consensus of the Club members, usually hashed out openly over cocktails and card games at what came to be known as the Round Table.

The Board also doubled the size of the practice range, and replaced piles of discarded railroad ties with a lighted par-three practice course. The new facility was a particular benefit to the Club's children, who were playing an increasingly important role in the social life of the club. The pool was packed with kids all summer – Bob and Marilyn Deichert's sons were the first two members of Golden Valley's swimming team – and families always stopped at the Club to and from trips downtown. The increase in family participation coincided with a surge in adult golf participation.

For decades, the Club's two big summer events have been Valley Days – a member-member competition – and Golden Days (member-guest). The Club annually shut the course down for two days so the maximum one hundred and twelve teams could play the Golden Days event.

"The demand to get in was unbelievable," said Jim Vieburg, who won Golden Days in 1975 and 1981, and teamed with Jim Scheller to win Valley Days in 1980. "You had to get to the club at 7 a.m. Saturday morning to get in, and it was filled by 7:30 a.m."

"The 1951 group were all businessmen, all on expense accounts, and they all retired at the same time," said Rick Rendahl. "If you wanted to play at seven o'clock Saturday morning, and you called in, you wouldn't get in. You had to stand in line. We had so many events, it was incredible. All of them were sold out."

The switch from a Shriners club to a country club hadn't changed the fun-loving atmosphere at Golden Valley. "In the early days nothing could have changed the Club, because it had such character," said Judy Pihlstrom, who joined with her husband, Dick, in 1967. "When we went to the Club it was our entertainment. We wore long gowns, we dressed up, people smoked in the clubhouse, and everybody went to the parties. There wasn't such a thing as people going south for the winter, so that was our entertainment there."

Despite the sustained enthusiasm, there wasn't enough money on hand for necessary capital improvement projects at the time, including a new roof for the clubhouse, a new golf course watering system and the three-hole practice area. The Club increased men's golf dues from $70 to $100 per month, passed a food and beverage minimum, initiated a new crackdown on delinquent member accounts, prohibited members from consuming their own liquor on the premises when the Club bar was open, and once again eliminated honorary lifetime memberships.

Though golf membership fell to 340 by the end of the decade, the Club's finances had stabilized once again. During John Sieff's presidency, all but one of the club's 375 golf members voluntarily contributed $200 for an injection program that saved many of the elm trees on the golf course from Dutch Elm disease. Golden Valley is one of the few Minnesota courses that has been able to retain a number of specimen elms that give the course character and definition.

The Club also planted hundreds of trees as a hedge against losing more elms. So many were planted on the right side of number fifteen at the bottom of the hill that they eventually had to be thinned out. "We were able to save quite a few, but we planted too many," Bruce Smith said. "Now we're taking them out, trying to get sun to the roughs."

Jim Scheller

If Jim Scheller's golf experiences had been limited to his two-year blaze of glory in 1990-1991, he would have been a happy player indeed.

In 1990, the Golden Valley dentist won the State Senior Open, a remarkable accomplishment for the four-handicap golfer who had never won a significant championship and was known as something of a renaissance man, a former jet fighter pilot and paratrooper with deep interests in science, literature, writing, hunting and fishing. A year later, however, he astonished both himself and the rest of the Minnesota golf world when, at age fifty-two, he held off two of the best players in the state's history, John Harris and Tim Herron, to win the 1991 Minnesota State Amateur at Minnesota Valley.

Jim Scheller
Courtesy: GVGCC

Scheller probably would not even have entered the '91 Amateur had he not received an exemption for winning the Senior Amateur the previous year. He had not attempted to qualify for the State Amateur for several years. He told the Star Tribune, "I didn't feel I really belonged in a tournament like this. It means taking a day off work to try to qualify, and then three more days off to play in the tournament itself. And I don't really feel like I have had much of a chance to win. Not against all these college kids with their flat bellies."

Nobody shared that opinion after Scheller's 7-under-par 66 – a round that included holing a 100-yard sand wedge shot for an eagle two on the 345-yard thirteenth – gave him a five-stroke lead after the first day. He took a four-shot lead over Harris into the final round after an even-par 73, and finished with a 74 to claim a three-shot win over Harris and Herron.

"A constellation of things had to happen for me to win," Scheller said after the victory. "And they all did. By far, that was the most fun I've had in golf, and the best thing that's ever happened to me in golf."

Scheller might have wanted to reassess that pronouncement a decade later. If the stars aligned to help him win the 1991 State Amateur, they sprinkled stardust all over him on Sunday, May 19, 2002: He made a pair of holes-in-one during a single round at Golden Valley.

His first ace came on the 170-yard fourteenth hole. "It was like a dream sequence," said Scheller. "The first one happened so quick it startled me. Then when we got to seventeen, [playing partner] Dick Kenny said to me, 'Here's your chance to get two.'

"I said, 'Wouldn't that be something?' I could see it hit nice, and when it rolled in, we all went nuts. It was like a circus." He had aced both of the holes before, but the odds against acing them in the same round were sixty-seven million to one.

Scheller had been a grinder in his thirties, obsessively going over each round to figure out where he could have saved strokes or made better decisions. Eventually, however, he learned to relax, grab a club and hit his shots more spontaneously.

"The last few years I've tried to play the game with a more instinctual approach," he said as he pursued his State Amateur triumph. Once Scheller learned to relax and have fun on the course, the results were spectacular.

Fortunes really began to turn around by the mid-eighties, when the members approved a $300,000 capital improvement plan to remodel the clubhouse.

After years of tinkering and, in some cases, outright desecration, the golf course finally got some respect. In 1985 the Club hired noted golf course architect Geoffrey Cornish to create a plan to restore the course to Tillinghast's original design. The restoration was interrupted, however, when the City of Golden Valley and the U.S. Army Corps of Engineers informed the Club that a control dam – with five-foot-high berms on either side of Bassett Creek – would have to be built on the ninth hole as part of a project to prevent the creek from flooding farther downstream.

The initial plan would have ruined the ninth hole, but after several years of contentious debate and counter-proposals, Cornish helped craft a compromise that stabilized the creek bed, created alternative holding areas for the water and created a redesigned tenth hole that did not negatively impact the golf course. The Club received compensation which it used to drill a second well near number seven, giving the club two excellent water sources. In addition, the Corps of Engineers cleaned out all the overgrown brush along the creek to the left and behind the tenth hole and rip-rapped the creek.

One of those involved in the redesigned tenth hole was Bill Coggins, a former college golfer who joined the Club in 1981. Even though he didn't know anyone at Golden Valley, he liked the course. "I've always been attracted to the old classic-style golf courses," said Coggins. "I probably have three hundred books on the history of golf, and I've always been a student of the game. I wanted to learn more about it."

1993 Bird's Eye View of Golden Valley Golf Club
Courtesy: GVGCC

The Courage Center Benefits

Though Arnold Palmer's tournament-winning days were coming to an end in the eighties, he was still golf's King, and still commanded Arnie's Army wherever his travels took him.

They took him to the Golden Valley Country Club in 1983 and 1984, as the headline attraction for the Courage Center Benefit. Over the years, the event would also feature appearances by Chi Chi Rodriguez, Fuzzy Zoeller, Hubert Green, Peter Jacobsen, Tom Lehman, Doug Sanders, John Mahaffey, Charlie Coody, Doug Sanders, Dale Douglass and Bob Toski. But it was Palmer's appearances that are best remembered.

Arnold Palmer and Al Yngve
Courtesy: GVGCC

Based in Golden Valley, the Courage Center started in 1928 and later merged with the Sister Kenny Rehabilitation Institute, which opened in 1942. The organization was founded to bridge a gap in services for people with disabilities, and now serves clients of all ages with a wide range of diagnoses. The annual Courage Center charity event was Golden Valley Country Club's most notable fundraiser.

Bob Haig, a Town & Country member who worked for Penzoil, was going to donate money to the Courage Center. His wife, who volunteered at Courage Center, suggested he pay for all the carts and caddies and entry fees, instead of just giving money to the event. Haig did so, saving the charity thousands of dollars. Through Haig's Penzoil connection, Arnold Palmer was brought in for the first two years of the event.

"People would pay an extra thousand to play six holes with him," Don Fink recalled. "On the seventh tee, he would wait for the next group, and play the next six holes with them, and do the same on the last six holes. He'd play with twelve different people, paying an extra $1,000 apiece."

Fink said that meeting Palmer was exactly what he'd expected after hearing so many stories of Arnie's warmth with people. "What everybody writes about him, he's that kind of guy," Fink said. "He was past his prime then, but to this day he's not past his prime personality-wise. I drove along and watched, and I took pictures of him."

Fink photographed all the caddies with their participating pros, and mailed the photos to the pros to autograph for the caddies. "The first year, Palmer's caddie was Bill Kozlak," Fink said. "He wasn't very big. He picked up the bag, and it was kind of heavy. Somebody said, 'Get him a pull cart,' and I said, 'If he can't carry it, give it to someone else.'" Palmer took out his umbrella and his rain suit, and asked his small looper how the bag was now. "Lighter," the boy said with obvious relief.

Palmer wasn't the only one who charmed the crowds. "They were all gracious," Fink said. "Fuzzy bought a shirt, and when he was done he gave it to his caddie."

A lasting legacy of Palmer's Courage Center appearances is the name of the ninth hole, "Palmer's Lament." The story goes that he thought he had hit a perfect drive on nine, only to find to his dismay that his ball nestled in a right side fairway bunker that he either hadn't seen or thought he could carry.

JODY ROSENTHAL ANSCHUTZ

Jody Rosenthal Anschutz
Courtesy: GVGCC

Of all the golfers who learned the game at Golden Valley, no one had more success than Jody Rosenthal Anschutz. Born in 1962, Jody was the daughter of then-Golden Valley members Bud and Doreen Rosenthal. Jody must have inherited some of her ability from her mother, who won four Golden Valley women's club championships between 1979 and 1985. By that time, Jody was winning titles herself: While playing for Hopkins Eisenhower, she was the first girl to win three consecutive Minnesota State High School Championships, from 1979 through 1981. She also won three state Junior Championships.

During the summer after her senior year in high school, Rosenthal won the State Women's Amateur match play championship on her home course, defeating Anne Zahn of Town & Country. She would beat Zahn in the finals of the Women's Amateur the next two years as well, at Hazeltine and Olympic Hills.

Jody played college golf at the University of Tulsa from 1981-1985, and was part of a team that won the 1982 NCAA and AIAW national championships. She earned six individual titles while in college, was a four-time first-team All-American and had two runner-up finishes and a third-place showing at the NCAAs.

In 1984 she won the British Ladies Amateur and played on the United States Curtis Cup team. When Jody turned pro in 1986, she won LPGA Rookie of the Year honors. In her second season she won two tournaments including the du Maurier Classic, which was then one of the LPGA's major championships. Jody Rosenthal finished in the top ten in the other three majors and placed fifth on the money list. She married Fred Anschutz in 1989, and last played on the LPGA Tour in 2002.

Coggins got an education on club politics as the tenth hole project progressed. "I spoke against it at the meeting, but it passed," Coggins said. "We thought it was going to be a disaster, but it turned out once that hole was done, many of us look at it as a possible signature hole. It turned out beautifully."

Donavon Roberg, Club president at the time, told Coggins that he appreciated his input, and appointed him to the Greens and Grounds Committee. Coggins would play a more significant role in later course projects.

Bob Levy joined Golden Valley in 1987, along with other members who left Rolling Green Country Club [now Medina Golf & Country Club]. He was looking for a more mature golf course, and one that was more convenient to his home.

"The member who interviewed me said, 'We think of ourselves as a bunch of truck drivers who were successful enough that we ended up owning the trucking company,'" Levy said. "You have egos, but our membership is pretty down to earth and accepting of each other."

The old guard had its most significant clash over women's playing rights. As more women entered the workforce, it had become inequitable to continue to reserve prime tee times for men only. The state legislature passed a bill in 1986 that would take away a private club's favorable tax status if that club did not grant equal membership privileges to both spouses. As with many golf clubs in Minnesota, the Golden Valley Country Club was not in compliance.

A group of Golden Valley women golfers, led by businesswoman Nan DeMars, pointed out that women could not play on Tuesdays between 10:30 a.m. and 3:30 p.m.; on Wednesdays between noon and 3:30 p.m.; on Thursdays after noon; on Fridays between noon and 1:30 p.m.; and Saturdays and Sundays before noon. Junior golfers had more rights than women; they were allowed to play Saturday and Sunday mornings and Thursday afternoons.

Judy Pihlstrom was one of the women who advocated for more equitable starting times. "One time a foursome of us went out a little bit earlier on a Saturday," she recalled. "The men could see us from the locker room – we were just going down the first hole. They made Don Fink come and get us off the golf course, and there wasn't anybody on the course. We knew the rule, and we were pushing it a little bit." They had a friendly discussion with Fink, but they got off the course.

"When the ladies asked to have an audience before the Board, they weren't too welcomed," said Wally Christenson. "In that era it was thought of as a men's club. All the Shriners were men, and the women didn't enjoy nearly as much participation and kinds of governance that would give them equal rights."

Pihlstrom said it was difficult for men in those days to give up power. "And yet, as we know, clubs don't exist without women – they're kind of the social people, they make arrangements for dinner and everything else," Pihlstrom said.

The initial response from the Golden Valley Board was that spouses could have equal access to the golf course if they elected to pay dues equal to those paid by regular members. That decision did not comply with the legislature's intent. Golden Valley's Board then weighed the pros and cons of conforming to the law and allowing open play. The advantages would have been to preserve the tax credit and "get dissident groups off our back." The disadvantages, they believed, would be increasing the number of players eligible for prime tee privileges from 350 to 550 adults; possibly violating membership contracts by charging the same amount in dues for a more crowded course; an estimated loss of $152,000 in revenue; and getting "other dissident groups on our back."

Golden Valley became the focal point of an issue that was affecting most of the Twin Cities clubs, according to Christenson. "It raised quite a bit of hackles in the community of all the clubs in town," he said. "Each club would find itself challenged with legal complications if we didn't change our accountability to women for equal and fair treatment."

The Club was required to prove that it was complying with the new law by August 1, 1989. The Board considered non-compliance, which would have led to a $80,000 tax hike in 1990 – 2.5% of the club's annual expenses. The Board said it would have to reduce Club membership by ten percent, or thirty-five members, if it complied with the law. The cost would be $437,500 in initiation fees, and higher dues for the remaining members. Because the new law did not allow one spouse to elect to pay reduced rates for reduced access, the result of complying would be an increase of dues for most families, according to the Board.

Many Club members did not believe complying with the law would lead to such dire consequences, however. Ultimately, the question was put to the membership at a special meeting, and a solid majority voted to comply. On the deadline day of August 1, Golden Valley Country Club began allowing women members to play golf with the same access and privileges of membership as men.

1992 Minnesota State Amateur

Golden Valley's greens have long had a reputation for speed and treachery. Don't get above the hole, the experienced player will tell you, and that was never more true than in July 1992, when the Minnesota State Amateur returned to Golden Valley Country Club for the sixth time.

Defending champion Jim Scheller of Golden Valley spoke for most of the field when he told a Minneapolis Star-Tribune reporter, "These greens were the fastest in the sixteen years I've been a member here." Scheller's long putter did not save him from shooting a ten-over par 83 during Monday's opening round.

Only forty-six of the 156-player field managed to break 80. Leader Terry Moores III of Midland Hills used a long putter to shoot a two-under-par 71 and didn't three-putt a single green. Just three other players broke par with 72s; Edina's John Harris, a three-time State Am winner who would win the U.S. Amateur the following year, was another shot back at even par 73.

Tim Herron
Courtesy: Robert Gusick

"You have to have patience on a course like this," Harris said. "You have to keep the ball below the hole because there are some places where they had the pins today when you just can't be above the hole or you're going to three-putt or worse."

Moores followed his first-day heroics with an 85, while future PGA star Tim Herron, then an All-American at the University of New Mexico, tied the Golden Valley course record and the tournament single-round record with an eight-under-par 65 during Tuesday's second round. Herron's career-low round included eight birdies and an eagle. No one in State Amateur history had shot eight under during a single round. (Those who had previously shot 65 at Golden Valley were former assistant pro Bobby Tomlinson, former State Amateur and State Open champion Gene Hansen, and member Jay Swanson.) Herron birdied five of Golden Valley's six par-five holes and eagled the other one, the 533-yard eighteenth hole, which he reached in two with a 225-yard four-iron. His drives routinely carried more than 300 yards.

The spectacular round gave Herron a two-shot lead at seven under par over Harris, who made eight birdies during his second-round 68. Jim Scheller managed to make the cut, shooting a 75 to go with his opening 83, but the final round was a duel between Herron, then 21, and the veteran Harris, 39.

Herron's three-under par 70 in a steady drizzle was good enough for a State Amateur record ten-under par total of 209 and a six-stroke victory over Harris, who shot 74. Herron was the only player in the final-round field of sixty-six players to break par for the day. His lead was cut to one shot after the front nine, but a tap-in birdie on ten after a thirty-yard bunker shot propelled him to victory. Herron and Harris would be victorious partners the following year during the Walker Cup matches at Interlachen.

"The difference of opinion between golf members seems much less important than it did a few years ago, and the camaraderie that has long been a hallmark of our Club has returned," wrote President James Talmage in the club newsletter a year later. "It seems we succeed in spite of ourselves."

There were accomplishments by females at Golden Valley that everyone could cheer about during that period. Liza LaBelle, daughter of members Ron and Carole LaBelle, became the second winner of three straight State High School Girls' Golf championships, winning the Class A title in 1986, 1987 and 1988 while playing for Breck. She would go on to play for the University of Alabama.

In August of 1988, the Club hosted 207 young women from around the world for the U.S. Girls' Junior Championship. The final match was won 5 and 4 by 15-year-old Jamille Jose over Debbie Parks. Years later, Jose – now Jamille Lee – recalled arriving at Golden Valley to see all the USGA committee women in attendance. It was like having "100 moms" there, she told a USGA reporter. "They were so warm and welcoming," said Lee. "And seeing so many girls that were on that level of golf ... was almost overwhelming." Future LPGA star Brandie Burton was the medalist with a two-round score of 141. Jamille Jose defeated future two-time U.S. Women's Amateur champion Vicki Goetze, 3 and 2, on her way to her title.

The course record that Tim Herron tied at the 1992 Minnesota State Amateur stood up for just two more years. Tim Gonsior, winner of multiple Golden Valley Club Championships, fired a nine-under-par 64 on August 18, 1994. Gonsior, an insurance salesman, had come from Midland Hills in 1977 as a 10 handicap and spent more than a decade steadily improving his game as he learned the quirks of the Tillinghast course.

"Probably the best thing was learning how to play the course and learning how to control my temper," Gonsior said. "I learned how to move the ball from left to right and learned the greens. The real defense of the course is the greens. You had to avoid playing to certain parts of the green, depending on where the pin was."

Gonsior's lowest round had been "probably a 66 or 67" prior to that August day in 1994. Playing with friends Charlie Hvass and Jack Dobbs, Gonsior's round started with a birdie on the first hole that could have been an eagle had his ten-foot putt not stopped an inch short of the cup. That would be an omen; he missed a half-dozen birdie putts of six feet or less during his round.

Gonsior made the turn at four-under 33, and then eagled ten. He made his only bogey on the par-3 eleventh hole, but bounced right back with birdies on twelve and thirteen. "I knew pretty early that it was going to be a pretty low round, but I never thought it was going to be as low as it was until the 13th hole. Then I knew I had a chance to do something pretty special."

He was aware that 65 was the course record, but he didn't feel pressure, even after dropping his one long putt of the day, a downhiller on sixteen that got him to nine under. "I just felt really good," he recalled. "I knew what I had to do: Keep making birdies. I tried to, but I just missed on the lips. They all came very close."

Gonsior missed a "fairly makeable" birdie putt on seventeen, and stood on the eighteenth tee one shot clear of the record. He set himself up with another short birdie putt on eighteen that would have given him a 63, but that one just missed, too.

Though he no longer plays as often as he used to, Gonsior made another run at the record in 2012. "I shot 29 on the front side, but missed a number of opportunities on the back side," he said. "I thought I had it at that time."

While Golden Valley has produced many fine players over the decades, its former reputation as a high-buck gambling club has faded away, according to Jim Vieburg.

"We had the reputation for very high stakes games on the course," Vieburg said. "And there were dice games – the 4-5-6 game was huge – and poker games. We played every Thursday night, and it went on for years. Gambling on the golf course is almost nothing compared to what it used to be. The guys that gambled got old and died."

Bruce Smith said he used to stay at the Club until the early hours on a weeknight. "Now I'm out of there by six or seven o'clock," Smith said. "In this day and age there is literally no gambling, except with my Thursday group. When somebody in our group scores a hole-in-one everybody pays him two hundred and fifty dollars. Wait till the IRS hears. I've had three holes-in-one – that was when it was five hundred dollars from everybody. Golden Valley had some absolutely fantastic members, still does, and I gravitated toward those that have the most fun."

When the city resurfaced Golden Valley Road and put in a sidewalk, curbs and gutters in the early nineties, a tunnel was built between the fourth green and fifth tee, finally eliminating the danger of someone being hit by a car while walking to their next hole.

The clubhouse was once again in need of upgrading by then, but rather than refinancing the building, the Board asked members to voluntarily pay $5,000 apiece to cover long-range capital improvement plans. Though many felt a new clubhouse was inevitable, the plan passed by a 131-110 vote and the money went into a dedicated bank account.

A new program allowed prospective members to join for a small monthly fee that covered the months from August to the following March; at that time, he or she would have to decide whether to become a full member.

In 1998 the Club undertook the last phase of its fifteen-year golf course restoration project: the bunkers. From the opening of the Tillinghast design in 1929, the deep bunkers were the signature feature. Some thought the bunkers were simply too deep for daily play. Others believed the bunkers were a great test of golf skills, and set Golden Valley apart as a classic-era gem. Over the decades those bunkers had been altered – and in some cases removed – so often that it was difficult to recall the course's original features.

Removing sand as part of the 1998 bunker restoration project
Courtesy: GVGCC

"In the early fifties, it was an old Tillinghast-designed course with bunkers as deep, or deeper, than they are now," recalled Rick Rendahl. "They had ladders to get in and out. Then, as golf become more popular with television, they wanted to take an old golf course and make it look like a new golf course, like Wayzata. It never would be Wayzata – I caddied there. They tried different things to make it a contemporary golf course, but despite good intent, it didn't really work."

Prior to the 1998 restoration, bunkers such as these on the 18th green were much shallower than Tillinghast envisioned
Courtesy: GVGCC

By 1998, the golf world had rediscovered the genius of the old masters – Tillinghast, Ross, Raynor, Mackenzie, Flynn, etc. – and was urging restoration of their great golf courses. Golden Valley Country Club realized that its most valuable asset was its A.W. Tillinghast course, and the best way to celebrate that asset was to restore the bunkers to their original shape, size and depth.

"The biggest problem we had with the bunkers was flashed sides," said Bill Coggins, who had become chairman of the Greens and Grounds Committee. "I used to say if a flock of geese flew over and urinated in them, they would wash out. It would take three or four days of labor to rake the sand up the faces. The bunkers held water, and there was no drainage. The first thing was a utilitarian need to rework the bunkers. They were just not playable, and costing too much time with all the washouts."

Coggins and Superintendent Mike Olson looked at the plans drawn up by Geoffrey Cornish in the eighties, and then went around the course hole by hole, identifying where old bunkers had been and where current bunkers needed to be restored to their original contours and intent.

"I was always a huge classic fan," Coggins said. "I wanted to go back to the old way if we could." Coggins, Olson and general manager Craig Surdy put together a handout for the members, detailing what was to be done, and the explanation and history behind the proposed changes.

"We did a lot to educate the membership before we put it to a vote," Coggins said. "We had opposition. Some people were a little skeptical – one member who's been there forever has always been against everything. But the final vote was 22 out of 355 members against."

The Club hired Tillinghast restoration specialist Ron Forse to recreate Tilly's bunkers as closely as possible. Using old photos, the Club knew that the bunkers originally had grass faces and flat bottoms, but the desire to "modernize" the course in the early sixties caused the Club to change the bunkers to sand-faced in order to improve their visibility on approach shots. Tillinghast built subtle berms around the bunkers to keep rainwater runoff from entering the traps, but those berms eventually came to be considered decorative "chocolate drops." Most were removed or allowed to wear away over the years.

Ron Forse's 1998 efforts clearly re-captured Tillinghast's original efforts
Courtesy: GVGCC

"Golden Valley has some of the most dynamic grass-faced bunkering ever done, about as strong a set of bunker features as Tillinghast ever did," Forse said. "You cannot pigeonhole and stereotype A.W. Tillinghast. He varied his work tremendously. In the same year he did deep pot bunkers at Somerset Hills [in New Jersey], he was doing sand flashing and grass faces in California. He did all kinds of things. He flashed sand up a lot, and brought sand down a lot. He was an individual on each site. It's hard to tell what made him do what he did at every location."

Forse and contractor Jeff Hartman studied old photographs and aerials to determine the outline of each bunker to be restored. "The photographs were absolutely priceless to tell what should be done there," Forse said.

A shaper carefully seeks out the original bunker bottom
Courtesy: GVGCC

While digging around each bunker for signs of its original contour, Hartman discovered that there had been three separate bunker alterations, revealed by the layers of dirt and sand that were found, beginning with a layer of rich yellow sand used by Tillinghast in 1926. Hartman and Forse ignored their preconceptions of the original shapes and excavated each bunker to the exact size and depth indicated by the lowest layer.

"Some were complete surprises, having been deeper and moved several feet," wrote Surdy in his project summation. "One was even several feet into a green. Each was restored as originally constructed."

The original project budget was $400,000, and did not include reinstating bunkers that had been removed. "We had the money," Coggins said. "All our debt had been retired. We paid for it totally out of cash flow."

Calling Golden Valley "an exceptional effort by one of the century's very best architects," Forse believed any deviations from the original design would only weaken the integrity of Tillinghast's masterpiece. As new information turned up, Forse advised the club to return every bunker to the original depth and reinstate all removed bunkers. The Board eventually approved the following:

- A new tee on hole number eight.
- A restored right front bunker on hole number two.
- An added berm to the rear of hole number five.
- Draining bunkers to the creek on hole number six.
- Moving the right fairway bunker farther from the tee on hole number nine.
- Restored two rear bunkers on hole number twelve.
- Restored the left greenside bunker on hole number fifteen to two bunkers.
- New berms to left and right greenside bunkers on hole number sixteen.
- A new berm to greenside bunker on hole number seventeen.
- Bunkers that once existed on holes one, two and three were not reinstated.

"One thing Tillinghast liked to do was those large mounds behind bunkers," Forse said. "They helped delineate the green site, and you'll notice that they pop up at various points, never mechanically, so you can tell where the outside of the bunkers are and get a target. He wanted you to know there were bunkers out there."

The original plan did not include the tenth hole because it had been remodeled during the flood control project in 1993, but when it became obvious the hole would be glaringly out of character with the rest of the course, the Greens & Grounds Committee recommended that the bunkers there be restored.

Coggins lived close to the course and stopped by twice a day to watch the work in progress. "It was fascinating how that project was done," said Coggins. "When we started opening up the bunkers, we found a bunch of stuff. There was a member back in twenties and thirties who smoked cigars with a plastic tip and always threw them away on the course. We found a bunch of them on the first hole."

Once the newly restored bunkers were put in play, the course absorbed a 5-inch rainfall in May, but none of the new bunkers washed out or became contaminated with dirt.

"We have less chance for plugged lies," said Wally Christenson. "Sometimes in the past that would end up leaving an impossible shot. I remember one time when Arnold Palmer got to the fourteenth hole and had a pretty nice round going. He put a ball underneath the lip of the sand trap, and had to extricate it so it would fall down deeper into the trap. He took a double bogey. I'm sure it was exasperating for him. The design is such now that we've tried to prevent those kinds of unwelcomed lies in the sand trap."

The bunker faces were mowed at a height of three inches to minimize the number of balls that came to rest in the grass faces. The bunkers can still present an unwelcomed lie, but of a different nature. "You get that transition edge at the bottom," said Bob Levy. "Anybody who gets that lie at the edge, they say, 'I was Cogginized.'"

"I guess that's my legacy," Coggins said. "Even the new members pick up on it pretty quickly. When a new member comes in, the old members will say, this is the guy that's responsible for getting all this done. I was chairman, but we had a lot of great people working on the project."

Even Coggins admitted that there are quirky lies against the back edge of a bunker, or sidehill lies when balls don't roll down the banks and into the bunker as they should. But he doesn't mind. He believes that the Golden Valley bunkers now play more like the Scottish-style pot bunkers Tillinghast admired – sometimes requiring that a shot be hit out sideways or backward, rather than toward the hole.

"It's a hazard," Coggins said. "Is the penalty too much for average players? I don't know. People get excited once in a while with a bad lie, but with flash faces, you could get buried in the face so deep you couldn't see it. It can be a harsh penalty, but if you hit it in the water, that's harsh, too. It's given our course a lot of interest."

"If you have a wife five feet tall like I do, you'd never find her in there," John Sieff said of the restored bunkers. "They'd never get out. They're pretty deep."

"I like them," said multiple Club Championship winner Jerry Gruidl. "I think they're a penalty, and bunkers should be a penalty."

"Some of the bunkering now might be a bit too narrow in spots, but for the most part they tried to restore them," said Tim Gonsior. "Once you learn how to play these, most bunkers don't give you any sort of problem whatsoever."

Along with restoring the bunkers, in 1998 the Club once again changed its name, to the Golden Valley Golf and Country Club. (In 2001 the club considered changing its name to The Tillinghast Golf and Country Club, to more firmly tie the club's identity to the famed architect who designed its course. After looking into the legal issues, however, the club decided to stay with its current name).

Jerry Gruidl

Jerry Gruidl
Courtesy: GVGCC

When Jerry Gruidl was thirteen years old, he hitch-hiked from his home in North Minneapolis to the Golden Valley Golf Club to caddie. "That helped me get into golf," Gruidl said. "I used to like to get a loop with the guys who teed off first thing in the morning, so we'd be done in two and half hours. It didn't pay very well, but I could hitchhike over to Wirth [Golf Course] and chip and putt. I sure did learn."

What he learned at Golden Valley helped him become one of the best players in the state. He played four years on the Minneapolis Henry golf team and won the Upper Midwest Bronze Amateur at Wirth in 1963. His first statewide victory came in the State Publinks Championship at Wirth in 1972.

Gruidl's family moved to New Hope, but he joined Olympic Hills instead of Golden Valley because the Club still required new members to be Shriners. After the requirement was dropped in 1971, Gruidl joined Golden Valley Country Club. And he won even more tournaments, including the 1977 State Four-ball with Bob Wernick, and the Resorters Tournament in Alexandria, where he beat a young Tom Lehman in 1977.

"My win up at the Resorters was a good one – he [Lehman] was just coming out of high school, just going to college. He made a comment later, 'If I could compete with a golfer like Jerry Gruidl, I can compete against anybody.'"

Gruidl was tough to beat on his home course, winning the Golden Valley match play club championship ten times between 1973 and 1999, and the stroke play championship four times. He was nearly as good at the state level: Gruidl won the State Senior Amateur Championship in 2000 and 2002, and the Players' Championship in 2001 and 2004. He and partner Bob Leaf of Hazeltine won the State Senior Four-Ball Championship in 1999, 2002 and 2007. He was named the MGA Senior Player of the year in 1999, 2000 and 2002. "I played in the U.S. Senior Open in 2000 in Saucon Valley," Gruidl said. "I was second or third in line to play [the U.S. Senior Open] at Des Moines [in 1999], but no one canceled."

Gruidl considers it one of his greatest feats to have played in the U.S. Amateur and U.S. Mid-Amateur when he was fifty-four in 1998. He was a week too young to play in the U.S. Senior Amateur that year. He lost in the second round of the Mid-Amateur to two-time champ Tim Jackson, and missed the cut in the U.S. Amateur at Oak Hill by a couple of shots.

In 2010 he won the Masters Division of the State Senior Amateur Championship. "Jerry could play," said former head pro Don Fink. "He was probably a better tournament player than regular player because he liked the atmosphere. He's good under pressure. In a tournament, he was as good a partner as you're going to find. Some guys are better at it, some go the other way. He was better at it."

"I've heard that," Gruidl said, when it was suggested he played his best when the pressure was greatest. "That, to me, was what you always had to do. When we were kids, we'd play for quarters just for the competitiveness."

The Tillinghast name does attract new members. Mike Monahan joined Golden Valley sight unseen after moving to the Twin Cities in 2004, because he was a fan of Tillinghast golf courses.

"I think he's one of the preeminent designers of all time," Monahan said. "I'd put him in the pantheon of amazing designers with Ross, Macdonald, Mackenzie, and more recently, Coore & Crenshaw and Tom Doak. All are somewhat minimalist designers who challenge every part of the game. With Tillinghast, you have to hit a draw on one tee shot, a fade on another, have a good short game and a steady hand with the putter."

Monahan has played many Tillinghast courses around the country, and his interest in golf course design led him to serve on the Club's Greens and Grounds Committee for six years. During that time he worked with chairman Mark Zeman, Pete Rasmussen and golf course architect Mark Mungeam on a master plan for the future of the course. Monahan believes Golden Valley's green complexes are superior to any other course in the Twin Cities, citing the small, subtle, back-to-front sloping greens with no humps and intimidating bunkers.

"The best approach shot we have on the golf course is hole number twelve," Monahan said. "It's one of our stronger and most underestimated holes. It's a great driving hole: Keep it on the right side of the fairway and you'll get a good bounce that will lead to a good approach. But if your approach is off in any way, you're in trouble. You only have to go in those bunkers once to know you don't want to be there again."

Monahan is an advocate of more tree removal on the course. He says hole twelve has been substantially improved since a storm blew down two big oak trees that used to overhang the green. "A poor shot into that green had as good a chance of ricocheting onto the green as into a bunker," Monahan said.

Monahan's favorite hole is number fourteen. "That is one of the best par threes I've ever played," he said. It calls for a mid-iron shot threaded between bordering trees and deep greenside bunkers, with "no margin for error, and no day at the beach when you get on that green."

Ryan Nelson, a member since 2009, grew up playing Hazeltine and the other top Minnesota courses as a Junior PGA and high school golfer, and calls his home course the best he's played in Minnesota. He was "floored" upon discovering the Golden Valley course and the favorable terms for younger applicants to become members.

"I hadn't seen it, and I couldn't believe it existed," Nelson said. Nelson said Golden Valley has holes where you can gamble and holes where you must play position golf, which allows players to develop all aspects of their game. It is typically wise, on classic old courses with steep back-to-front greens, to keep your ball below the hole, but it's so true at Golden Valley that Nelson calls it "laughable." The greens play smaller than their actual size for strong players like Nelson, a two handicap. He has to try not to spin shots off the front of the green while intentionally landing short of the hole. "That's where it works on your game a bit," he said. "You have to take that into consideration and hit a shot with less spin."

Nelson plays in some statewide events and calls it "a confidence booster" to play most of his golf at Golden Valley. "When you play other courses, they seem a lot easier. Putting on our greens is so much more involved than it is at other courses. Reading breaks, reading speed – that helps a lot. It's nice to play such a tough course, then go to other courses and feel relieved."

"In all these years there are places I've played out of where I think to myself, 'I've never been here before,'" Judy Pihlstrom said. "It's a wonderful course. I hope it remains one."

The most recent golf course upgrades involved putting in a new irrigation system and renovating the tees. There was resistance from some members who feared the changes would merely create a longer, tougher golf course, but a majority of the new tees were created for seniors. For the better players, the longer tees allowed the course to be played at 7,000 yards, which restored the approach shot values that Tillinghast originally intended. That has allowed the Club to attract good young players, including a group of long-hitting hockey players that includes New York Islanders forward Kyle Okposo.

The club also installed family tees for adults to play with their younger children. Jim and Donna Hawley, members since 2011, spend a large amount of their golfing hours at Golden Valley with their seven-year-old grandson, who plays off the family tees. "When they added the [family] tees, that was a big bonus," said Donna Hawley. "We're not die-hards; we play more for enjoyment."

The new clubhouse after the 2002 renovations
Courtesy: GVGCC

The clubhouse that opened to such fanfare in 1958 had undergone renovations, expansions, repairs and upgrades almost from its grand opening, and forty years later, a majority of the club members had grown weary of constantly being hit up for a new round of remodeling. Beginning in 1995, the Board began weighing a number of proposals.

The controversial clubhouse project in the early nineties remodeled the downstairs grill adjacent to the men's locker room, but now the Club was having issues with heating, cooling, and leaks. The locker rooms were old and dingy, with five or six little cubbyholes, exposed pipes and old metal lockers. The only kitchen was upstairs, so the cooks used a dumb waiter to get food to the downstairs grill, which had a limited menu.

The choices were to build a new clubhouse, or remodel again – at a cost of eight or nine million dollars. They looked at building both a huge clubhouse with lots of banquet space and a smaller option for members and smaller golf events only, along the lines of the new Spring Hill Golf Club in Wayzata.

"I was of the mind that it was a lot of money, risky for the Club, and we should update the old clubhouse," said Bob Levy. But after looking at the finances, Levy became an advocate for the new clubhouse. "The problem is you lose all your grandfathering status. You have to bring the old clubhouse up to code. You'd do it for less, but you'd still have a design that was fifty years old."

"Even when we finished we'd still have an old building as far as infrastructure," Coggins said.

"I'm tall – 5'-11" – and my husband's taller," said Roberta Mellen. "Walking down the hall to get to the grill in the old clubhouse, we had to stoop over a bit. The hallway was extraordinarily low. Just the thought of putting in a new clubhouse was controversial – not just the assessment, but people didn't believe there was a need. It was sentimental; people had so many good times there, they couldn't imagine it being razed. But both for the fiscal health and culture of the Club, the Club would have died without the new clubhouse."

The issue became not whether to build the new clubhouse, but how big it should be. In 1999, long-range planning co-chairs Alan Meuwissen and Andy Weiner led town hall meetings that gave everyone a chance to provide input about what features were needed to satisfy the current membership as well as future members. Members who complained were asked to join the committee.

"What we were building was what the collective community wanted us to build," Weiner said. "Compared to other clubs around town, there wasn't an individual personality who rammed home what it was or wasn't. It was the collective mind that ended up with the spaces we had."

Because of the desire to have a big enough space to hold its Valley Days and Golden Days events, the Club proposed to build a 60,000 square foot clubhouse, at a price tag of $13.5 million. Member approval was not a foregone conclusion, though. At the time, clubs like Oak Ridge, Edina and Minnesota Valley had seen clubhouse proposals go down to defeat, some multiple times. Coggins said that, prior to the vote of the membership, the Board agreed that if the clubhouse plan didn't pass by a significant margin, they would do something else.

"We wanted to have a nice majority," Coggins said. "We knew we were going to have a big assessment and take on debt, and at the time the club was debt free. We got ours right through on the first ballot. We had a huge turnout."

The membership approved the new clubhouse in 2000, Coggins' last year as president, by a margin of seventy percent in favor. The biggest point of opposition was the banquet facilities for outside events.

"My directive was that if we're going to do this, I want this clubhouse to have a lot of things for the membership," Coggins said. "The biggest bone of contention was with the locker room. We'd have fifteen-inch lockers, half lockers – I was totally opposed to that. I said, 'No, we're not going to do that. If the members are going to spend $13.5 million to begin with, they've got to get something out of it. I want the best locker room in the Twin Cities, with full eighteen-inch lockers made out of the nicest wood – a first-class situation. Without that, I won't support the project.'"

The construction started in August 2001 and continued during the winter. The site of the original clubhouse was the highest point in Golden Valley, but when the old clubhouse was razed, the hill was leveled by fifty feet. The new clubhouse sat just south of the old building's site and was extended out to the swimming pool on the east side. During construction, a temporary pro shop was built above the cart storage building where the practice putting green is now.

"We used the old clubhouse for a good part of the year, and when they pulled the whole building down, we moved our facilities into the pro shop and the cart storage area," Coggins said. "We lost the locker room, but we used some trailers. It seemed like it went awfully fast. We played out of the pro shop, had sandwiches and drinks, then we went to Schuller's [Tavern]

The Ridgewood Bar
Courtesy: GVGCC

if we wanted to do something else. It worked out really great. It was a fun time. Watching that building being erected was exciting."

The new clubhouse, designed primarily by Rick Christiansen of the Twin Cities firm of Partners & Sirny, opened in July 2002. Located immediately adjacent to the eighteenth green, it included Coggins' first-class locker rooms, plus floor-to-ceiling windows that looked out over the eighteenth and second holes, exposed wood-framed beams, vaulted ceilings, gabled roof lines and rooms named for famous Tillinghast courses, including the Ridgewood Bar and the Bethpage Ballroom. There were separate front entrances for club members and outside groups, with capacity for up to seven hundred guests. It became the frequent site of weddings and receptions, social events and business meetings.

"I was opposed to the new clubhouse, like a lot of other older members. Why did we need a great big place like that?" said Al Yngve. "But it turned out to be a good idea. The banquet facility is busy."

"We went the bigger route, which meant we had to be in the banquet business," said Levy. "Outside events is the business model today. If you don't find a way to generate revenue from your fixed overhead, it's a burden. So it worked for us. Our large banquet facility subsidizes our golf membership. It does not take money away from members. It supports itself and throws something extra into the pot. It gives you a place for holiday parties, et cetera. I will tell you there were a lot of members who were opposed, and I can't say they were wrong, but the club would be different. It would be a golf club like Windsong Farm, just closer in."

The outside golf events often leave the course a bit worse for wear, according to membership chairman Allan Share, who joined the Club in 2000, but superintendent Jeff Ische and his staff "do their magic" to return it to pristine shape within a day. "We love having the events," Share said. "It's great revenue for the club, and we know that a lot of people who would never get to experience Golden Valley get to play. We call it brand awareness. We're always pitching. People will go home and say, 'I played the greatest golf course today.' What price can you put on that?"

Main Foyer
Courtesy: GVGCC

Rick Rendahl said the larger clubhouse actually makes for a more intimate member experience during outside events. "It has made the private part of the club more private," he said. "I wasn't necessarily a strong proponent of it at the time, but the guys who did the heavy lifting, the core guys who put the thing together, did a heck of a job. I think it's going to continue to be a positive for the club in terms of growing and new members."

"Even today, when I'm playing with guys who've been there twenty-five or thirty years, they get on the eighteenth tee, look out and see the sun on the clubhouse, and someone always says what an amazing site it is to look up there and see that building," Coggins said. "People are impressed. Most people are proud to be a member with a building and facility like we have."

"They're going to live in that clubhouse for the next fifty years," Weiner said. "It's fantastic. It looks beautiful, it's functional, and sited well. I drive up and go, 'This is a gorgeous place, and I'm proud to belong. Proud to be part of it.'"

The Club's bylaws were rewritten during the first decade of the twenty-first century to allow women to serve on the Board. Up until that time, a membership controlled one share of stock. Most memberships were family memberships, and that share was held by the male. Since Board members were required to be stockholders, women were de facto excluded from serving.

Roberta Mellen, who had joined as a social member with her husband, Brad Cosgriff, in 1998, didn't pay much attention to the voting rules at Golden Valley until after becoming a golf member two years later. "Once I started being active on the membership, clubhouse, interiors, finance and other committees, I started to realize that some of the people who are active and contributing members were not even shareholders," Mellen said.

She wrote a letter to the Board, asking to change the shareholder structure to allow both husband and wife to become full members. She got no response at first, but a few months later the Board offered to transfer her husband's membership to her. Mellen persisted, writing at least two additional letters to the Board over the next year and half, providing them with details of the membership structures from other clubs. Finally, the Board allowed the membership to decide whether each shareholder should have two votes.

"I don't think the board did it very easily, but I'm a tenacious person," Mellen said. "I stayed at it, conducted myself professionally, and I think the board members who had concerns about the structure are now my strongest supporters."

The change in shareholder voting passed on the first ballot. This change led to Roberta Mellen being the first woman elected to the Board of Directors at the Golden Valley Golf and Country Club, and then the first woman to become Club president. In 2009, the club again amended its bylaws to allow domestic partners to be shareholding members, whether opposite sex or same sex.

"I think having that membership structure change has opened up the club to the dual income professional members, as many families are today," Mellen said. "When it was one person, one share, it developed out of the historical framework of 'men work, women stay home or at the pool.' This reflects a more contemporary society."

"We, as a membership, have come a long way," Coggins said. "I was heavily involved there for ten years when we did a lot of things that turned out to be successful."

After serving as president, Coggins turned his attention to captaining the Golden Valley Senior League team, but admitted to having some withdrawal symptoms over no longer being involved in the club's

GVGCC's First Female President, Roberta Mellen
Courtesy: GVGCC

decision-making. "But I've been very pleased with the way the club has carried on. I'm as pleased and happy today and I was in 2000 when we turned up the first shovel of dirt for the clubhouse, or in '98 when we finished the bunkers."

"My wife is not from here, but I grew up here, and by and large our dearest friends are people we met at Golden Valley," Bob Levy said. "I think that community atmosphere is part of it. This club has an incredible amount of volunteerism. The members are active in their community, with international charitable organizations and local charitable organizations."

Tom Jarzyna

Tom Jarzyna with Arnold Palmer
Courtesy: GVGCC

Tom Jarzyna has run the men's locker room at Golden Valley for decades, but that only scratches the surface of his importance to the club.

"There isn't a member at that club that couldn't tell you something special that Tommy had done for someone," Bob Levy said. "He's a neat guy – I don't know if he's the longest serving staff member, but he's the most loved. I don't think there's a finer human being on the face of this earth."

Jarzyna met some of the personnel of the Minnesota Twins while shagging batting practice at Metropolitan Stadium, and began working in the Twins' ticket office in 1970. After graduating from Richfield High School in 1972, Jarzyna was offered the position of clubhouse attendant. He had a locker next to his boyhood idol, Harmon Killebrew.

"What more could a person ask for than to see the names 'Killebrew' and 'Jarzyna' on lockers next to each other?" Jarzyna said.

In 1976, he was offered a job with the Seattle Mariners and was planning to move to Seattle the following year. While he waited, he took what he thought would be a one-year job at Golden Valley Golf Club and also met the woman who became his wife. He decided to stay.

"I was thinking that being married and working in baseball wasn't a good life, with all the travel," he said. "I felt sorry for the married people who worked with the Twins. I realized I couldn't live that way. I'm still with my wife, so it worked out in my favor."

It worked out in Golden Valley's favor, too. Over the course of thirty-seven years, Jarzyna did a bit of everything, from handling the club's laundry facilities to dealing with problems at the swimming pool, the engineering department, and serving as project manager and department head. He eventually cut back on his responsibilities to the point where he was solely running the men's locker room.

He oversees a locker room staff of six to eight high school and college students. They keep the locker room clean, shine shoes and accommodate just about any member or guest request. They even prepare to make sports chit-chat. "It's really important for us to know the sports page each day," Jarzyna said. "I want the members to come in and feel like they're at home. We're taking care of them, whatever it takes. Everyone demands something different, and I know what they like. It's important to know their family, their children's names and their grandchildren's names."

Jarzyna said he has the biggest family in town. "You become very close to everybody. I've met the members, their friends and their guests, I know as many people in town as anybody. I would do anything for anybody there, and most people would do the same for me."

Jarzyna has had his devotion to the club reciprocated in many ways, perhaps most tellingly in 1990, when he contracted Lyme's Disease. "I was pretty much bed-ridden for six months, most of the golf season," Jarzyna said. "They never batted an eye. They said to take care of myself. There was no financial or medical pressure on me to get back there. When I'm not there, it's noticeable, but they worried more about me than the job."

Jarzyna plans to work at Golden Valley at least until he'd been there forty years. "If I go forty years, I'll be happy. Maybe then I'll do something different. I've been well taken care of with kindness."

As the club enters its second century, Rick Rendahl believes Golden Valley faces challenges to keep its membership strong, young and viable, but Golden Valley is not alone.

"Every golf club, including Interlachen and Minikahda, has taken a look and said it's hard to get a thirty-year old kid to drop $75,000 to $80,000 and pay six hundred a month in dues for no equity," Rendahl said. "Younger members that have young families, they've got to have reason to decide this is where we want to be, what we want to do. I think they've done a good job with our young membership. We've got a lot of good, young guys playing. I think the exodus from golf has started to halt. It took us a while, but they've done a good job lowering the price, and now it's going in the other direction. I, as a member and previous president, feel good that we've got the basis set for the push forward. I've never seen our golf course this good."

Golden Valley's caddie program is as old as the Club itself, and remains vital entering its second century. The club has produced thirty-six Evans Scholars over the years; in 2013, three of the twelve Minnesota caddies receiving Evans Scholarships came from Golden Valley. Andy Weiner, Western Golf Association director of the club, emphasizes to both the caddies and their parents that a combination of good grades and excellence at the golf course can lead to a free college education. The Club's proximity to urban Minneapolis makes for a diverse group of candidates.

"A big part of the criteria is need," Weiner said. "Kids who caddie aren't just kids who love to be around golf, but also kids who have never picked up a golf bag and have heard other kids have made money caddying. It's a great job. You're learning the game, being industrious, and you can get a scholarship. We have a proud legacy of putting a number of men and women through college."

Golden Valley had eighty caddies in its program in 2013, with more than half getting regular loops. Beginning caddies attend clinics run by the caddiemaster during their first few weeks, and Weiner and several other members devote time on weekends to mentor the young people on-course. They must pass a written test on rudimentary aspects of the game, and once they finish the weekend seminars, they take an on-course test. Then the novice caddies do "shadow loops" with an experienced caddie.

"Once they can handle a bag, they're turned loose," Weiner said. "Two scholars this year are young ladies that never played golf in their life. They decided they could use the extra income. They found it fun, worked their butts off, and both are going to school on scholarship."

The bonds formed on the golf course remain strong at Golden Valley, though the groups and games change over time. Club attorney Mike Tewksbury, who joined in 1993, and Tim Gonsior play with a group of twenty-five men on Thursday afternoons. They'll play foursomes or fivesomes, organize a game amongst the groups, toss in ten bucks, and then divvy up the winnings and tell the stories during the chef's Thursday night barbecue.

Ryan Nelson plays with a group that enjoys sitting around the fire pit adjacent to the eighteenth green after a round. "We place small bets on the people coming up the fairway, how many shots will it take them to finish, what's the over and under – just having fun. It's quite the pastime."

Mike Monahan has a regular group that plays Wednesdays, Fridays and Saturdays, and when there's an opening, there's a line of players willing to take the spot. They always play a net game, so abilities will range from single digits to twenty-handicappers.

"I've always tried to make sure I get out and play with different folks," Monahan said. "In any given season I'll play with fifty or more players, guys and women, too, and engage in substantive conversations with them. But a majority of my rounds are with three of my best friends."

Henry Orme

At thirty-nine years, Don Fink is the longest-serving pro in Golden Valley's 100-year history, but Henry Orme is gaining on him. He was Fink's assistant pro for seventeen years and began his thirteenth year as head pro in the club's centennial year of 2014.

Orme found his longevity easy to explain. "It's a good club to be at, or I probably would have left a long time ago."

Like Fink, Orme is a St. Paul native, graduating from Highland Park Senior High. He got the golf bug early, getting his first job at age ten as a practice range ball picker for head pro Terry Hogan at St. Paul's Town & Country Club. He moved up to caddying, then working in the bag room and cart storage, and eventually moved into the golf shop.

Henry Orme
Courtesy: GVGCC

"Watching Terry Hogan do his job at Town & Country, I decided at age thirteen or fourteen that's what I wanted – to go into the golf business."

After one year of college classes at St. Thomas, he knew he didn't need college to pursue his goal. He worked for two winters at a club in Sarasota, Florida, and for three summers he was at Island View Golf Club in Waconia. He moved to Golden Valley as Don Fink's assistant in 1985, and succeeded him in 2002.

Orme doesn't get to play much golf – like his predecessor – but running the golf operation on a daily basis has allowed him to observe the changes at Golden Valley over three decades.

"Definitely when I first came here it was a men's club," he said. "Women did play, but the times they were allowed to play the course were restricted. Even after 1989, it was a man-dominated club. Even after the rule [to allow women to play on Saturday morning] was passed, a lot of them still didn't; whether it was their choice or their husband saying something to them, I don't know."

In the next fifteen years, however, Orme noticed that women started playing more, while men became more involved in their family life, including attending their children's sports events and school activities.

"Back in the old days, men went to work, came here and played golf, had a couple of drinks and went home. It's different now. Even though the growth of golf has stalled, more women and youth are involved, and that was a good thing. To grow the game, we offered a lot more programs for women and children. That's where you needed to go to get people to come to your club – more family activities, like holiday parties and special dinners."

Orme said total rounds were down about 3,500 per year over the past decade, and he estimates that has a lot to do with both spouses out in the workforce.

"What I see now is people having to work more hours, and not coming out as much," Orme said. "The times when people play have also changed. The tee sheet would be busy from 11:30 to 2:00, and now it's busy from 2:30 to 4:00."

Orme says there are good young players at Golden Valley, which is a good sign for the future. Jesse Bull, who qualified for the U.S. Mid-Amateur championship in 2011 and 2013, won the 2013 club championship with a two-round total of nine-under par. The course is a challenge for the longest hitters, with the blue tees now stretched back to 7,004 yards. The course has also accommodated older and novice players by building more gold tees, from which the course plays 6,007 yards.

Players are allowed to play the gold tees in events if they're at least sixty-five years of age and the addition of their handicap to their age equals eighty or more.

"That's made the game more enjoyable for them, and it has added participation to our events."

Orme witnessed significant changes during his tenure, including the 1998 bunker restoration project. "I've had a number of Golf Digest raters come to rate the course who've seen Tillinghast courses around the country, and they're always impressed with the bunkering we have here," Orme said.

The new clubhouse has made it easier for the Club to host large outside events, which bring in revenue that subsidizes the golf club. "We do have more outside events," Orme said. "A lot of clubs started hurting for membership seven or eight years ago, and all were looking for additional revenue. [The new clubhouse] gave the membership something to show off to others. Members are proud of it, and they're happy to show it off and bring their guest."

Orme sees his responsibility as doing whatever he can to get more young people playing the game of golf, so the future of Golden Valley will be as vibrant as its past. "I think the job for us is we have to continue to promote the game and get more people out and enjoying their golf course – making the club someplace where the family wants to come and spend some time. Our membership is getting younger, and we're a more family oriented club."

"You can get on the tee sheet with almost any group teeing off, and they'd say, 'We're glad you joined us'," said Allan Share. "It doesn't matter whether it's men or women. People don't show any compunction; they just join up."

Judy Pihlstrom remains a dedicated eighteen-hole player. That was the goal for most women in years past, with women remaining in the nine-hole league just long enough to get their handicap to thirty-six or below, qualifying them to play in the eighteen-hole league. But time – or lack of it – has decreased migration from the nine-hole League. "Now that doesn't happen," Pihlstrom says. "Some people play nine holes forever."

A small group of four to six women plays eighteen holes early Saturday mornings, teeing off at 8 a.m. "We were met with suspicion when we started about seven years ago," said Roberta Mellen. "There's always a Saturday game the pro shop runs. They've asked us if we wanted to get in the game, but we're not making a statement. We just want to get out and play and then get on with our day. We play fast."

Jim Vieburg recalled telling Charlie Hvass that the change in tee-time restrictions would not affect things very much – men would still play Saturday mornings, and women would not.

"But of course, that's changed," Vieburg said. "I look out there on Saturday and my wife's playing. When I joined, we had literally no tees for the women. They were playing at the same tee boxes as men. Maybe at the front, but there were no tees for them – 'If they don't like it, they can stay home.' It's been a change for the better. A lot of guys play with their wives now, and only with their wives. My health has been so bad, I know how some of them feel. I'm embarrassed – I'm playing so miserable compared to how I used to, that I'm playing with my wife more. But I'm seventy-eight and still playing. I gotta be thrilled I'm still playing."

With overall golf participation numbers down in the United States, and the creation of more high-end public golf facilities, the private country club model may be a tougher sell to a new generation. Yet Golden

Valley continues to attract younger members like Ryan Nelson, who had never been a member of a private golf club before joining Golden Valley in 2009.

"Growing up in a small town, the kids on our public course always beat up on the country club kids," Nelson said. "I never really wanted to be a part of that 'country club' label. But at Golden Valley, no one really wears that badge. The camaraderie feels just like the public golf course I grew up on in Albert Lea. The gate to pick up beer across the street at Schuller's – what stuffy country club in the metro allows you to do that?"

Nelson appreciates not feeling like he has to "walk on eggshells" at Golden Valley. "Everyone has respect for what it is, and everyone stays in line, not due to any authority, but out of common respect," he said. "It sets us apart from other clubs. Everyone there seems like they're there to play golf and eat good food."

Even those who don't play a lot of golf find that the Golden Valley version of the country club model works for them. Jim and Donna Hawley were like Nelson: At one time they wouldn't have seen themselves as country club types; they even saw private club membership as carrying a bit of a stigma. But Golden Valley provides what they're looking for.

"We didn't join to be able to say we belong to a country club," Donna Hawley said. "We joined mainly for sociability and to play golf at a nice course close to our work and home. The last two years we brought my parents from Canada to the Club for Mother's Day. We've taken part in a lot of activities for our grandson – swim lessons, golf lessons, junior golf camp, and the sledding party. The social part is just as important to us. It's given us an extended family."

The Hawleys' daughter Kea got married at the Club in the summer of 2013 – to Max Bull, brother of club champion Jesse Bull. The Hawleys felt extremely comfortable working with the kitchen and catering staffs at the Club, where everyone knows them by name.

"That's what's going to be part of the success of the Club in the future, those kinds of events that they put on for families and young families," Jim Hawley said. "That's where the growth is going to be. The strength of the Club will be those other amenities, along with golf."

"It's like my second home," said Allan Share. "Whether, golf, dinner or just a drink at the bar, we run into people we know and it's always like going home. I can't imagine how many other private clubs I've been to – some espouse what we do, but for the most part, it's not country club life the way we live it at Golden

A second home for many...
Courtesy: GVGCC

Valley." "Tillinghast is the reason I joined, but the people are the reason I've stayed," said Mike Monahan.

Wally Christenson, who came in as a young Shriner in the 1960s, enjoys seeing a new generation enjoying the Club. "What a blessing for the Club to have new young members who are the ongoing life of the Club," he said. "You have to have that to have a membership that makes a club strong. I think we're in a wonderful position right now."

... and a breathtaking setting as well.
Courtesy: GVGCC

PART SIX ❧
THE GOLF COURSE

A.W. Tillinghast's Golden Valley golf course design turned eighty-five years old at the same time the Club was turning one hundred. It is fully mature, fully restored, and the repository of some of Minnesota's greatest golf memories. The course's evolution can be followed by comparing photos of its early days to the images from today.

"The growth of trees has become much more than in the pictures of the original Tillinghast design," said Wally Christenson. "They were in their infancy then. They have contributed to defining and narrowing the fairways and making the course more difficult."

"They kind of got away from what Tillinghast did in the mid-to-late fifties," Jerry Gruidl said. "It was probably a great golf course then, but you didn't hit it as far. I told the architect, 'We don't need to change any of the greens, all we need is length.' By and large, the greens are just about everything I remember. I don't think you can get Golden Valley's greens real fast, because they'd be unplayable – the slope is just too much. Because I played Golden Valley, when I got to those [tournament] courses, they didn't intimidate me as much as they intimidated a lot of people. I kind of knew what to expect when you got behind the hole. When I beat Tom Lehman at the Resorters, I had a downhill ten-foot putt for birdie. That original green at Alex was pretty sloped, but it didn't surprise me when I made it. It probably surprised Tom."

Road Par 5
511 - 469 - 452 - 426

1

"I'm playing early in the season, and I hit a nice drive up number one. Then I shanked a ball; it went high up in the air, and out of bounds. I hear 'Bam!' and I know it hit the windshield of a car going down Golden Valley Road. I can't see it through the trees, so I walk over, and no car stopped, but I know I hit a car. I call up to the clubhouse and tell them if someone comes in with a broken windshield, tell them I hit a car, but nobody stopped. We finished our round, we go into the 19th hole, and there is Steve Schanz, a member of Oak Ridge who I've known my whole life. He says, 'Thanks for hitting my car.' He was coming to play golf at our club. They told him in the lot that it was me, and said he'll be in the 19th hole later. What are the odds? I've never put a ball out of bounds on the first hole since then."

Member **Allan Share**

"A beautiful starting hole; requires two fine shots for a birdie. Out of bounds all the way on right side and trees on left. Green guarded on both sides by deep traps, nothing short, and long grass over. Gives you a chance to miss a shot and still get a par. Should be quite a few eagles made on this hole."

Harry Cooper
September 4, 1943

"A short par five to start your round with OB down the entire right side. A drive down the left center would be ideal, giving even the average length hitter a chance to get home in two. Not a difficult hole to start out with as long as you stay left."

Henry Orme
February 13, 2014

GOLDEN SUMMIT PAR 5
556 - 526 - 491 - 446

2

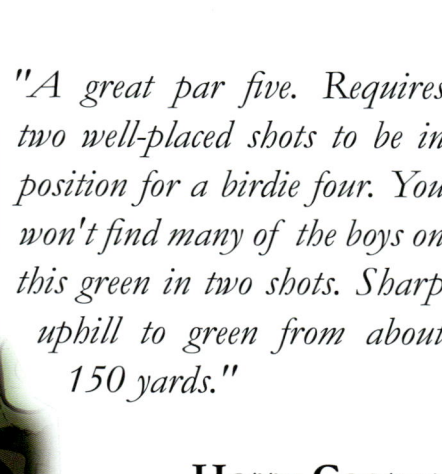

"Another par five that plays as a three-shot hole for most golfers, as only the bombers can reach this one in two. The key to this hole is the approach to the green that requires an accurate shot to an uphill green that is severely sloped from back to front. Don't be short on your third shot. Par is always good here."

Henry Orme
February 13, 2014

"A great par five. Requires two well-placed shots to be in position for a birdie four. You won't find many of the boys on this green in two shots. Sharp uphill to green from about 150 yards."

Harry Cooper
September 4, 1943

"One of the more fun things to do is to watch somebody hit a shot from behind hole number two, knowing more than likely they're going to be grabbing their wedge and taking a seventy-yard hike to their ball."

Member **Ryan Nelson**

Westward Ho! Par 4
426 - 375 - 356 - 321

3

"One of the toughest holes on the course to birdie as second shot to green is blind and very deceptive. Requires straight tee shot. Out of bounds all along left side of fairway to green."

Harry Cooper
September 4, 1943

"*Generous off the tee, this par 4 is all about the green - a typical Tilly design - that is severely sloped from back to front. Always take one more club for your second shot, but keeping the ball beneath the hole is your best chance at a good score. Even the best of putters can look foolish on this green.*"

Henry Orme
February 13, 2014

Gate Par 4
339 - 324 - 312 - 290

4

"Shortest par four hole on the course. Dogleg to right, out of bounds on left side all the way to green and over. Green bunkered on three sides, open in front. Well placed drive should put player in position for birdie. See lots of birdies here."

Harry Cooper
September 4, 1943

"Dogleg right par four that gives the players a risk reward option off the tee. Long hitters can take a rip at the green but must hit a high tee shot over the trees to get close. Trouble looms left as OB runs down the entire side for the players bailing from the trees on the right. The flattest green on the course makes any shot on the green a makeable putt."

Henry Orme
February 13, 2014

"When they redid the hole they had to put the gate back in, to duplicate what was there. Bud Pyre, one of our members, paid for it so he could go over to Schuller's and get something. He's passed away now — a great guy. He was a real character who played a lot. If any employee had a problem, he was the first guy to take up a collection."

Member **Don Fink**

TIERS PAR 3
168 - 161 - 153 - 147

5

"This par three is not that long but requires an accurate shot to hold this green. Two deep bunkers gobble up anything short and right, and another pit catches anything deep and slightly left. You can bail short and left of the green for the conservative play."

Henry Orme
February 13, 2014

"A great one-shot hole. Will be played from five-iron to four-wood, depending on wind. Usually played with four iron. Bunkered on right and back of green. Small opening to green. Will see few birdies on this hole."

Harry Cooper
September 4, 1943

Creek Par 5
491 - 467 - 442 - 377

6

"A good tee shot down the middle will give players the option of trying to carry Bassett Creek in two shots, while the shorter hitter should lay up on this par 5. A real risk and reward hole that can be taken advantage of if the tee shot is placed properly."

Henry Orme
February 13, 2014

"This hole requires a perfect drive to put you in position for a great second shot for an eagle three. Should see lots of birdies on this hole and plenty of trouble. Out of bounds on left side and creek across fairway. Green guarded by deep traps. Front open. One of the most interesting holes on the course."

Harry Cooper
September 4, 1943

"My favorite hole is number six because I scored a double eagle on it. I hit three wood to the top of the hill and had about 210 yards in. I hit five-iron to the back pin placement. Standing on the top of the hill, we saw it hit, bounce onto the green and start to track toward the hole. A couple of us started yelling 'Go in!' and that's when it disappeared.

The guys behind us came up to us on hole eight and asked if that's what happened, because we were all yelling and screaming. We told them, 'Yeah.' They asked me where the ball was. I had already teed off on eight, and I was still playing with the ball. They said, 'You should probably take that out of play.' Thankfully, I didn't send it out of bounds or into the water, which I've done many times."

Member **Ryan Nelson**

RESPECT PAR 4
445 - 422 - 352 - 315

7

Golden Valley Golf and Country Club

"On seven, the fairway was boggy, like a peat bog, and spongy. You'd hit a shot and your ball would be down in the grass. Eventually they tore the fairway up and put matting underneath it. They did a good job. That made it a lot better."

Member **Al Yngve**

"This great par four is the number one handicap and for good reason, as it demands a long tee shot and a forced carry over Bassett Creek on the second to have a birdie putt. Bunkers surround a sloped green which makes par a great score."

Henry Orme
February 13, 2014

"Long dogleg. One of the best par fours on the course. Very few birdies will be made on this hole. Deep rough on left, woods on right off tee. Creek runs across fairway in front of green and deep traps on three sides. Front open."

Harry Cooper
September 4, 1943

Island Par 3
209 - 170 - 150 - 117

8

"Shortest hole on course. Should see lots of birdies on this hole. Creek in front of tee and traps on three sides of green."

Harry Cooper
September 4, 1943

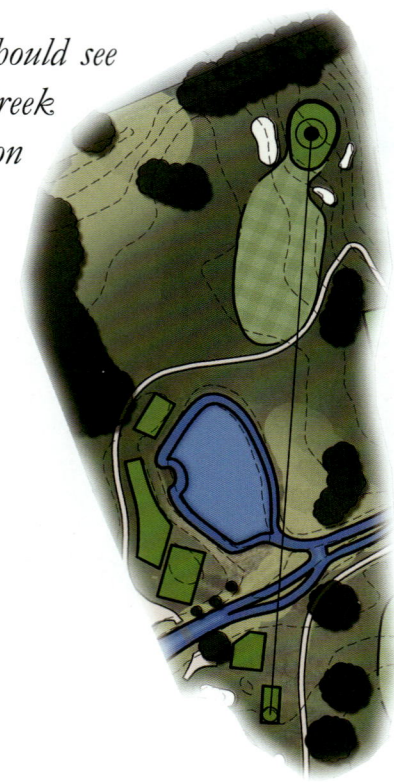

"A medium to long par three with a small, false-fronted green requires an accurate shot as bunkers catch anything slightly to the right and left. Missing the green on this hole makes for a difficult up-and-down as the surface is sloped and the ball can run away from you in a hurry!"

Henry Orme
February 13, 2014

PART SIX: *The Golf Course*

"I was playing with my friend Bill Nelson when he got a hole in one on the eighth hole. We were teammates that day, and I made a birdie on that hole. We're walking to the ninth tee and somebody in our group said we got a Lawrence Welk: A one and a two."

Member **Mike Tewksbury**

Palmer's Lament Par 4
432 - 382 - 354 - 329

9

"Out of bounds on left off tee. Very deceptive second shot. Green well guarded on three sides. Elevated green. Will see birdies on this hole."

Harry Cooper
September 4, 1943

"Bunkers right and left will catch a stray drive, so keep it down the middle on this par four. Your approach to a slightly elevated green that is sloped from back to front with bunkers right and left makes an accurate shot a must. Keeping the ball slightly below the hole is recommended on this one."

Henry Orme
February 13, 2014

PART SIX: *The Golf Course*

"I made an eagle on nine, playing for a fair amount of money. One of the guys I was playing against was in the group ahead of us. I think I hit a four-iron into the cup for a two. The person in front of us was Ted Wangenstein. I came off the green and said, 'I just made an eagle.' He wasn't too happy about it; he said, 'Yeah, I saw it.' "

Member **Al Yngve**

CORNER Par 5
536 - 504 - 443 - 420

10

PART SIX: *The Golf Course*

"*Dogleg. Best par five on the course. Out of bounds on left. Creek runs across fairway and winds up along left side from about 190 yards to green and around back. Requires two great shots to get on this green.*"

Harry Cooper
September 4, 1943

"*A great par five entices the longer hitters to give it a shot in two as a long tee ball over the left trees will give you a look on the second shot. A creek that runs across and along the left side of the hole must be carried, and might not be worth the risk. A lay-up will give you a fairly straight forward approach to a green guarded by bunkers right and left.*"

Henry Orme
February 13, 2014

"*My ball had come to rest on the bridge on ten, and it looked like the shot to play. I took a swing and fell off into Bassett Creek. I drifted under the bridge and lost my glasses. My friends have put a plaque on the bridge; fortunately it's not the Mike Tewksbury Memorial Bridge. It could have been, when you look at the rocks below. Whenever I'm in a group with someone who hasn't seen the plaque, I have to explain what happened. We never found the ball. Figuring out what happened to the ball was not a high priority.*"

Member **Mike Tewksbury**

"Not a long par three by today's standards, but this green is sloped from back to front and has bunkers waiting for the errant tee shot."

Henry Orme
February 13, 2014

Valley Par 3
173 - 153 - 137 - 113

"A fine par three hole. A bit deceptive playing to elevated green. Not much trouble on this hole."

Harry Cooper
September 4, 1943

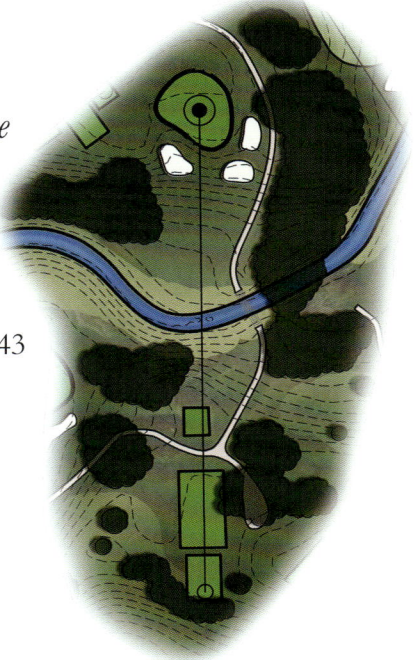

PITS PAR 4
408 - 395 - 379 - 332

12

PART SIX: *The Golf Course*

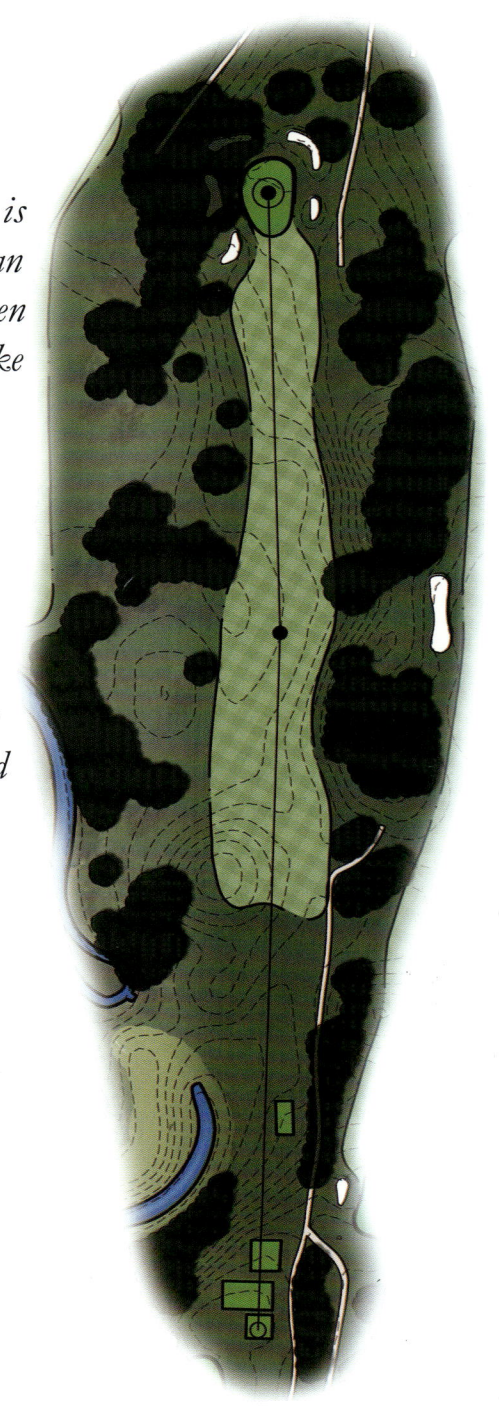

"Generous off the tee, this par four is all about the approach, demanding an accurate shot to a slightly elevated green surrounded by deep bunkers that make for a very tough sand save."

Henry Orme
February 13, 2014

"Fine par four. Good tee shot here to be in position for opening to green, guarded on three sides by deep traps."

Harry Cooper
September 4, 1943

Dick Sawyer, who grew up on the Golden Valley course, chipped in for an eagle three here en route to shooting the lowest first-day round — an even-par 73 — in the 1931 Trans-Mississippi tournament.

REDEMPTION PAR 5
491 - 468 - 456 - 411

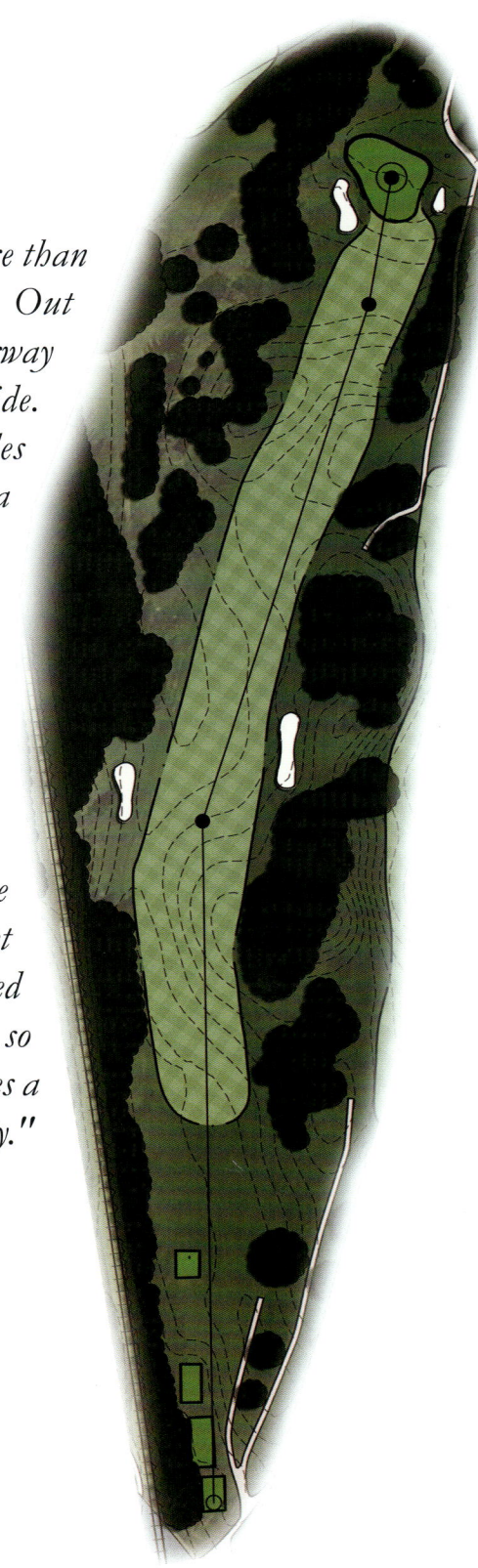

"This hole will be birdied more than any other hole on the course. Out of bounds to the left of fairway and bunkered on right side. Green trapped on both sides by deep traps. Good hole for a few eagles."

Harry Cooper
September 4, 1943

"Here's a par five that even the average length player can get home in two. This green is sloped severely from back to front so being just below the hole provides a great birdie or eagle opportunity."

Henry Orme
February 13, 2014

"Steve Finkelstein, a good friend and a member, never saw his hole-in-one on fourteen, He was busy talking, bending down, getting his tee. And there's an addendum: Most guys put the ball away after a hole-in-one. Steve hit his out of bounds on the next hole."

Member **Allan Share**

NARROWS PAR 3
180 - 165 - 140 - 136

"Maybe the tightest par three in the state as this narrow tree-lined hole provides many challenges. A long, narrow green with deep bunkers and out of bounds long, it may be best played from the front of the green with a hopeful two-putt."

Henry Orme
February 13, 2014

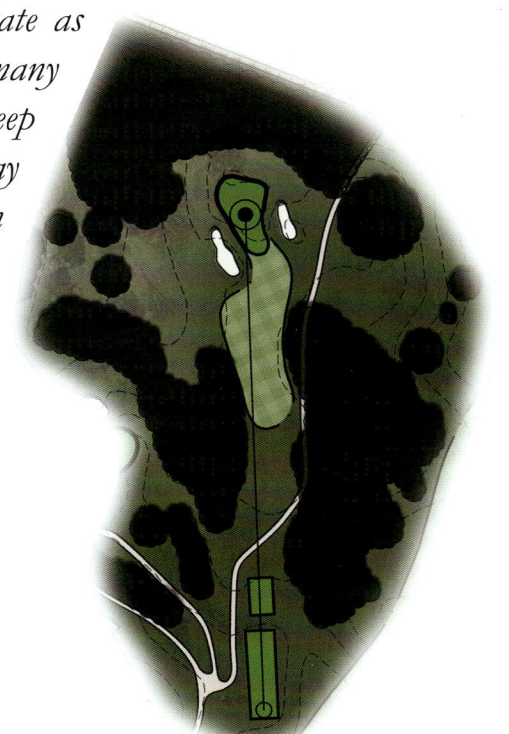

"Beautiful par three hole. Traps on both sides of green require about number five to number three iron shots, depending on wind and player."

Harry Cooper
September 4, 1943

"During Valley Days, this guy I'm playing with is ready to hit his second shot, down at the bottom of fifteen, when a helicopter came over low. I don't know why. The noise was loud, everybody looked up, and the next thing I knew, the ball wasn't there. I said, 'What happened?' He said, 'I hit it and it went in the hole.' I said, 'You're kidding! Weren't you distracted by the helicopter?' He said, 'What helicopter?'"

Member **Jim Vieburg**

Railway Par 4
432 - 402 - 375 - 343

15

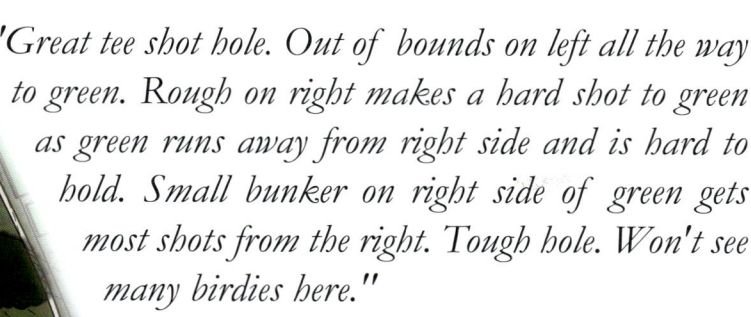

"Great tee shot hole. Out of bounds on left all the way to green. Rough on right makes a hard shot to green as green runs away from right side and is hard to hold. Small bunker on right side of green gets most shots from the right. Tough hole. Won't see many birdies here."

Harry Cooper
September 4, 1943

"This slight downhill par four has out of bounds down the entire left side. Par can become a difficult task when it is easy to want to "bail right" off the tee, where a forest of trees awaits. This green has typical Tilly bunkers guarding it with a back to front slope which makes a putt from below the hole the key."

Henry Orme
February 13, 2014

Tim Gonsior holed a long downhill putt here for a birdie during his course-record round of 64 — the only long putt he made during the round.

Steeple Par 4
448 - 413 - 391 - 319

16

"A great par four. Best hole on course. Long hitters can cut off quite a bit of dogleg and shorten hole. Second shot to elevated green and partly blind; very deceptive. Very few birdies here. Green well guarded by deep traps. Bad over as green slopes away and hard to hold shots from back of green."

Harry Cooper
September 4, 1943

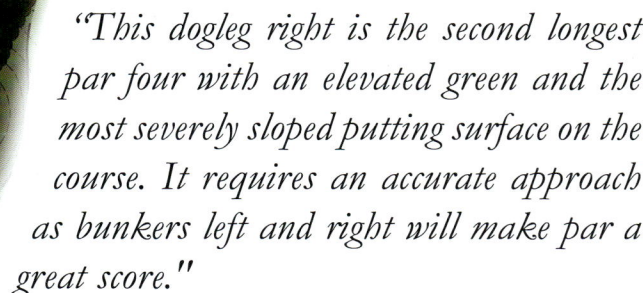

"This dogleg right is the second longest par four with an elevated green and the most severely sloped putting surface on the course. It requires an accurate approach as bunkers left and right will make par a great score."

Henry Orme
February 13, 2014

"When we re-did the pond on seventeen in 2007, we re-did the timber retaining wall. It went from where the green was all the way around to the other side of the pond. John Essell was playing in the fall with friends when he hit his tee shot into the pond near a flock of ducks. John hit his flop shot onto the green, which startled the ducks. The last duck took off, cleared the retaining wall, but couldn't see John. He strikes John in the back of the neck, hits him on the nerve, and John is knocked out cold. If somebody had yelled 'Duck!' what would it have meant?"

Member **Bob Levy**

WISHING WELL PAR 3
185 - 162 - 145 - 126

17

"A fine par three. Very deceptive shot. Green slopes toward tee. Trapped on both sides, very narrow opening. Bad over as hard to hold shots coming back onto green."

Harry Cooper
September 4, 1943

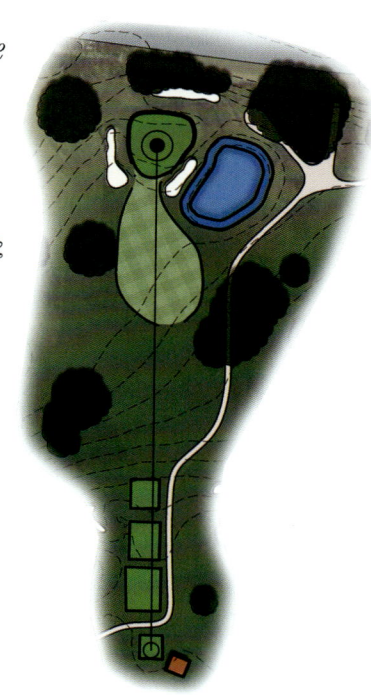

"Water looms right as this downhill par three will test your iron play. Bail left and a big bunker awaits as this back to front sloped green is a challenge in itself. Being just short of the green is a conservative option."

Henry Orme
February 13, 2014

Tilly's Tavern Par 5
574 - 528 - 499 - 439

"This longer par five will require three shots for the modest player. A bigger than normal green that is well bunkered makes the approach the key to this hole. The green is sloped and best played from slightly below the hole, as most of Golden Valley's greens demand."

Henry Orme
February 13, 2014

On the final day of the 1943 Golden Valley Invitational, Toney Penna capped a run of four back-nine birdies with a four-footer on eighteen to prevent the team of Byron Nelson and Jug McSpaden from winning the tournament. Les Bolstad blasted a second shot that finished just off the green here during his record best-ball round with Joe Coria in the 1944 Golden Valley Invitational. He chipped it next to the cup and made the putt for the 59.

"A great long finishing hole. Long hitters will have a chance to get home, if wind is behind, with two long shots down right side of fairway as that is shortest way. Big trap in front and short left. Only grass bunkers around green. Should see birdies on this hole."

Harry Cooper
September 4, 1943

CLUB PRESIDENTS

1916-1917	Hendrick Booraem	1978-1979	Gordon Engstrom
1918	John Burgess	1980	J. Robert Nygren
1919-1921	Jean Hartzell	1981	Gary Persian
1922	Arthur C. Statt	1982	Oris A. Hendrickson
	C.R. Sievers	1983	Charles W. Guptil
	E.S. Mooers	1984	Thomas C. Tsatsos
	S.O. Abrams	1985	LaRoy Luther
1934	Austen S. Cargill	1986-1987	Joe Burkard
1935-1936	E.P. Kehoe	1988	Richard Rendahl
1937-1938	George C. Wright	1989-1990	James Talmage
1939	Paul J. Schmid	1991	Gene Smiley
1940	Elmer Bates	1992	Donavon Roberg
1941-1946	E.W. Cameron	1993	Harry Vakos
1947-1949	Guy E. Masters	1994-1995	Richard Henry
1950-1954	Ray C. Ewald	1996-1997	Alan Meuwissen
1955	Maurice H. Graham	1998	Rick Boe
1956-1957	Paul C. Johnson	1999-2000	Bill Coggins
1958	Myrl Fairbanks	2001	John Tsatsos
1959-1960	Carl Jensen	2002	William F. Nelson
1961-1963	R. Algert Johnson	2003-2004	Tom Kozlak
1964-1965	Charles R. Erickson	2005-2006	Brian Liesch
1966-1967	Charles H. Vrooman	2007	Bob Levy
1968-1969	Blair Merwin	2008	Kevin Aasgaard
1970-1971	E.W. Nelson	2009-2010	Roberta Mellen
1972	Charles T. Hvass	2011	Scott Bullock
1973	David Arneson	2012	Tom Shannon
1974	Lawrence Rosenthal	2013	Al Boston
1975	Charles R. Coulter	2014	Jim Brown, Jr.
1976-1977	John P. Sieff		

CLUB MANAGERS

1917-1928	J. Cliff Miller
1929-1937	H.O. Piffner
1938-1940	A.C. Harvey
1941-1944	Arthur C. Statt
1945-1946	Norman C. Iverson
1947	C.E. Arnold
1948	George K. Gammon, Jr.
1949	Dell V. Carlson
1950	H.R. Bell
1951-1954	Serio Rossi
1955-1957	Thomas Borden
1958-1961	Bill Bell
1962-1964	Hans Lefeber
1965	Hans Schubert
1966-1967	Tony Kallas
1968	Arne Gunderson
1969	Owen Bjornson
1970	Joe Sochneki
1971-1973	Carl Weiser
1974	Serio Rossi
1975-1983	Glenn Gustafson
1984-1985	James Amundson
1986-1988	Bernd U. Sturm
1989-1993	Christopher Chapman
1993-2004	Craig Surdy
2004-2010	John Swaney
2011-	Francisco Gonzalez
	Jeff Ische
	Tom Rubenstein

HEAD GOLF PROFESSIONALS

1916	Elwood Queen
1917	Walter Andrews
1918	Otis George
1918	John Dryburgh
1919	Cyril Walker
1920-1926	Otis George
1927-1935	Bim Lovekin
1936-1937	Pat Sawyer
1938-1941	Ray Keller
1942-1944	Harry Cooper
1945-1946	Les Bolstad
1947-1963	Harold Sieg
1964-1969	Joe Sodd
1970-2001	Don Fink
2002-	Henry Orme